Innovative Interventions for Today's Exceptional Children

Cultivating a Passion for Compassion

Anthony Scannella and Sharon McCarthy

ROWMAN & LITTLEFIELD EDUCATION
Lanham • New York • Toronto • Plymouth, UK

Published in the United States of America
by Rowman & Littlefield Education
A Division of Rowman & Littlefield Publishers, Inc.
A wholly owned subsidiary of The Rowman & Littlefield Publishing Group, Inc.
4501 Forbes Boulevard, Suite 200, Lanham, Maryland 20706
www.rowmaneducation.com

Estover Road
Plymouth PL6 7PY
United Kingdom

British Library Cataloguing in Publication Information Available

Library of Congress Cataloging-in-Publication Data

Scannella, Anthony.
  Innovative interventions for today's exceptional children : cultivating a passion
for compassion / Anthony Scannella and Sharon McCarthy.
      p. cm.
  ISBN-13: 978-1-57886-869-8 (cloth : alk. paper)
  ISBN-10: 1-57886-869-6 (cloth : alk. paper)
  ISBN-13: 978-1-57886-870-4 (pbk. : alk. paper)
  ISBN-10: 1-57886-870-X (pbk. : alk. paper)
  ISBN-13: 978-1-57886-941-1 (electronic)
  ISBN-10: 1-57886-941-2 (electronic)
  1. Problem children—Education. 2. Problem children—Behavior modification.
 3. Self-control in children. I. McCarthy, Sharon, 1956- II. Title.
  LC4801.S33 2009
  371.93—dc22   2008028821

⊗™ The paper used in this publication meets the minimum requirements of
American National Standard for Information Sciences—Permanence of
Paper for Printed Library Materials, ANSI/NISO Z39.48-1992.
Manufactured in the United States of America.

Contents

Preface

This book can be used to start making a difference in children's lives now, in any way that is comfortable to you. Chapters 1 through 4 concern themselves with the presuppositions and beliefs the authors hold to be most effective in generating and sustaining the Passion for Compassion approach to behavioral change.

We invite you to think of the first four chapters as a blueprint for the space in which interventions should be designed and applied. If you have worked with children for any length of time, you are keenly aware that today's exceptional students need exceptional approaches. Exceptional approaches require remarkable attitudes and flexibility on the part of parents and teachers. In these beginning pages, you will become more familiar with the mind-set the authors have found to be successful in initiating and promoting positive and long-lasting behavioral change.

Chapters 5 through 10 outline the actual interventions. The interventions themselves are then divided into more specific categories. As you look over the interventions, some will almost leap off the page for you as you imagine those children with whom you will first use these specific interventions. You may find yourself tucking other interventions in the back of your mind for use at a later date.

You may even use this book as a reference text, relying on it in a pinch, for those times when you get stuck and don't know what to do . . . and you find yourself turning the pages of this book looking for the best intervention to apply. Any way you choose to use this book will be the way that is right for you. We have had so many successes with different children that we know you soon will be having feelings of increased personal efficacy.

If you are a dreamer, have passion and compassion . . . read on. If you have children in your life with whom you just don't know what to do . . . read on. If you simply enjoy reading stories about children . . . read on. Finally, if you have ever said to yourself, "There has to be a better way than punishment and consequences" . . . read on. Sooner or later, you'll be grateful you did.

Acknowledgments

We gratefully acknowledge our colleagues, friends, and families for their unconditional support.

We especially would like to thank the many educators, parents, and students we have met over the years in workshops, trainings, and private practice. They have influenced our thinking, our learning, and most of all, our teaching. We celebrate you!

Great thanks to the Board of Directors and staff at the Foundation for Educational Administration, Inc. (FEA).

Thank you, Thomas Koerner, Maera Winters, and the staff at Rowman & Littlefield. Your suggestions and support throughout the process helped greatly.

Finally, to our families, who have been patient and tolerant, we are deeply indebted.

Introduction

Innovative Interventions for Today's Exceptional Children: Cultivating a Passion for Compassion provides teachers, administrators, and school counselors with an intervention framework for helping the struggling children in their lives. The focus of the Passion for Compassion approach is comprehensive and preventative rather than reactive and remedial. It is based on sound management practices rather than gimmicks and techniques. The purpose of Passion for Compassion is to assist in proper child development, both behavioral and academic.

The strategies and interventions, which are grounded in solid research and practice, include solutions for current issues that educators face daily. It is important to note that this text is a supportive professional tool, which will help all adults acquire the skills and knowledge necessary for them to be able to strengthen a child's capacity to function successfully and with resiliency.

In addition, educators following these strategies and suggestions will improve their relationships with their students and will have more fun on a daily basis. The authors hope that you find the information so valuable that you will share it with your colleagues and friends.

(A note about language: This book is addressed primarily to professional educators. We wholly believe, however, that a parent is not only a child's first teacher, but also his or her lifelong teacher. Therefore, this text is highly recommended for parents as well.)

The following metaphor, "How Are the Children," from *A Trainer's Companion* by Olsen and Sommers (2004), captures the beliefs and values of our approach.

> Among the many accomplished and fabled tribes of Africa, no tribe was considered to have warriors more fearsome or more intelligent than the mighty Masai. It is perhaps surprising then to learn the traditional greeting that passed between Masai warriors. "Kasserian ingera," one would always say to another. It means "And how are the children?"
>
> It is still the traditional greeting among the Masai, acknowledging the high value that the Masai place on their children's well-being. Even warriors with no children of their own would always give the traditional answer, "All the children are well."
>
> This meant, of course, that peace and safety prevail; that the priorities of protecting the young and the powerless are in place; that the Masai people have not forgotten their reason for being, their proper function, and their responsibilities. "All the children are well" denotes that life is good and that the daily struggles of existence, even among a poor people, include the proper care of the young and defenseless.

We wonder how it might affect our consciousness or our own children's welfare if, in our own culture, we took to greeting each other with the same daily question, "And how are the children?" We wonder if we heard that question and passed it along to each other a dozen times a day, if it would begin to make a difference in the reality of how children are thought of or cared for in this country . . .

We wonder what it would be like if every adult among us—parents and non-parents alike—felt an equal weight of responsibility for the daily care and protection of all the children in our town, in our state, in our country. Finally, we wonder if we could truly say without hesitation, "The children are well; yes, all the children are well."

What would it be like? If the president began every press conference, every public appearance, by answering the question: "And how are the children, Mr. President?" If every governor of every state had to answer the same question at every press conference: "And how are the children, Governor? Are they well?"

The authors know how hard you, the reader, work every day to improve the consistency of a positive answer to that question. In our humble way, this is our contribution.

Chapter One

Behavioral Change as Education

"Far more often we serve by who we are and not by what we know."

—Dr. Rachel Naomi Remen

Key Points:

- Behavior change is not about punishment; rather, it is about education, feedback, and self-control.
- Self-control is worth ten times more than self-esteem.
- Students have the resources they need to change.
- There is no such thing as failure, only feedback.
- If something doesn't work, do something else!

Do you remember the horse Secretariat? This legendary colt won the Triple Crown in 1973, the first horse to do so in twenty-five years. He won the Belmont, the third race for the Crown, by an amazing distance of thirty-one lengths.

A young reporter named Terry Hill was assigned by his newspaper to cover that specific race. There he was, a young man with a big assignment. He quickly found himself among the more experienced reporters, the ones with the big cigars and even bigger attitudes.

As Secretariat ran his astounding race, Hill found himself in the middle of electrically charged emotions. As he was settling into the knowledge that he had just witnessed history in the making and would have the austere responsibility of giving a written account capturing that moment, when even the extraordinary is transcended, in time, he looked around to share and capture this minute of his life with the legions of well-seasoned colleagues.

Imagine his surprise when he discovered that his fellow reporters, with their craggy faces, rumpled clothing, and tough-guy facades, were openly weeping—perhaps even unaware of the pure human emotion running down their smoke-stained skin. At this revelation, his hand reached up to his own youthful cheek to discover tears falling from his own eyes. Years later in his book, *Cafes are for Handicapping*, Hill explored a possible explanation for the emotional responses he and his colleagues experienced.

> Why do we cry when we see huge accomplishments? We weep for the Secretariat that is in all of us. In these poignant moments, we cry for the fact that there is something in us that could be every bit as great as what we are watching. We are that greatness in that moment. We weep because we know that our greatness isn't being realized.

As educators, our tears are twofold. First, we cry for our own frustrations and, just as often, we cry for those children who are not realizing their greatness. We are keenly aware of their potential for greatness.

You are certain that if only they would speak up, settle down, believe in themselves, plan for the future, or have some self-control, then these children could possibly reach their potential, the potential we see so clearly.

Like you, we have worked long and hard to find a way to assist these children. The approach we have found to work the best is a combination of education, positive feedback, and self-control training. We have found that the students who make better choices have a model in their heads, an imprint if you will, of what appropriate behavior looks like, sounds like, and feels like. Some students with ineffective strategies don't have these "imprints," while some students have them but can't retrieve them quickly. The interventions found in later chapters address these differing aspects of students' inability to choose appropriate behavior.

Many of the interventions found herein are useful in prevention. Some, like the ones in chapter nine that focus on setting and maintaining peak performance, are useful for helping children build self-control.

Still others work in concert with the students' brains, encouraging the students to rehearse and acquire new, more positive behaviors.

Furthermore, we believe that struggling children are not to be viewed as passive recipients; rather, they are active partners in a relationship. Through this collaborative partnership, the students recognize that *they* are responsible for their own behavior.

To take this thought further, consider yourself a consultant. The students have a problem (emotional, behavioral, academic, etc.) and as a consultant, you can collaborate with them to help put into action a plan that will change their lives.

To this end, the interventions in this book are written. They are not to be considered a series of "tools" that will automatically solve presenting problems. Rather they are to be considered strategies that you, as the consultant, can suggest in order to guide the student. Having expectations for the students is a sign that you respect them and that you believe in them enough to support them through change.

Here are some "consultant" guidelines to refer to when working with students:

- Consultants have expertise in the area where they recommend changes.
- Consultants elicit, clarify, and work toward the students' goals, not toward their (the consultants') own goals.
- Consultants are in charge of the process of consulting (establishing rapport, knowing the student's "model of the world," choosing appropriate interventions for the desired outcomes, and integrating change through the whole person); *the student is in charge of doing the change work.*
- Consultants operate within certain professional guidelines, such as confidentiality and sincerity. In return, they may expect their students to operate within appropriate guidelines, as set forth by both of them in the beginning.
- Together, then, you and the children work toward a desired state, always with the onus on them to do the work. Again, holding young folks accountable is a sign of respect.

One useful frame consultants use is that there is no such thing as failure, only feedback. When a student fails, it is a good opportunity for that student to know what not to do, what is useful, or how much more he or she needs to learn. That is good information, but it is not failure. This information feeds into the student's knowledge bank and can be framed as valuable, not a deficit.

Furthermore, effective change agents very often believe that everyone, every student, has the necessary resources (such as self-control, patience, diligence, and compassion) to change. This belief propels successful consultants toward an uncommon stick-to-itiveness, which they need to have in order to assist young people in their quest toward positive goals and behaviors.

Lastly, consultants thrive on flexibility. When something doesn't work, the savvy consultant tries something else . . . anything else. Trying the same intervention over and over without getting the expected results is futile at best. In any given situation, the individual who has the most flexibility has the most control. When a consultant, whether parent or teacher, works with students, flexibility should underlie all of his or her behaviors.

For your reflection:

What does it mean to be successful when working with struggling students?

What possibilities for student growth exist that we haven't thought of yet?

What kind of learning happens without direct instruction?

Chapter Two

Today's Exceptional Kids
Need Exceptional Approaches

"When we no longer know what to do we have come to our real work; when we no longer know which way to go we have come to our real journey. The mind that is not baffled is not employed. The impeded stream is the one that sings."

—Wendell Berry

Key Points:

- There is no such thing as a resistant student, only teachers or parents who don't have the requisite variety to help that particular child.
- Adults speak like adults.
- Change agents explore the students' phenomenological references— learning style, beliefs/values, and personality.
- The student makes new choices (the onus is on the student).
- Remember—don't get mad, get curious!

If you have students who you feel are exceptional, we are sure that you are going to find the information in the following chapters extremely worthwhile. The Passion for Compassion approach looks to mediate between caring teachers and struggling children. These children may be struggling behaviorally, academically, socially, and/or emotionally.

The following story, adapted from the Sufi tradition, frames our approach.

Once upon a time, there was a small boy who banged a drum all day and loved every moment of it. He would not be quiet, no matter what anyone else said or did. Many "wise wo/men" were called in by the neighbors and asked to intervene.

Lots of good ideas were proffered. The first wise person told the boy that if he continued to play the drum in that fashion he would break his eardrum. This reasoning was too advanced for the child, as he was neither a scientist nor a scholar. The second told him that drum-beating was a sacred activity and should be carried out only on special occasions. The noise continued. The third offered the neighbors plugs for their ears. The fourth gave the boy a book; the fifth gave the neighbors books that described a method of controlling anger through biofeedback; the sixth gave the boy meditation exercises to make him placid and explained that all reality was imagination . . . the noise continued. The seventh brought medication. The boy then thought he had a disease, and still banged on the drum.

Finally, an adult passionate about his efficacy with children came along. He looked at the situation, handed the boy a hammer and chisel, and said, "I wonder what is *inside* the drum?"

As you read and familiarize yourself with the Passion for Compassion approach, please refer back to this story. For instance, the young boy banging the drum may be any child in your life who has a consistently annoying behavior that has resisted the best you have brought forth to manage it. Or the story may remind you of a time that you wished you had just the right words to say to a hurting child.

Let us begin at the beginning. Young people learn from the behaviors they are taught, implicitly or explicitly. In other words, all behavior is learned. If a child is misbehaving, it is because someone taught or showed him or her how to misbehave. (Where did the boy get the drum?)

Once when we were doing a seminar, a parent came up to us during a break smoking a cigarette. His question to us, believe it or not, was, "How can I get my 13-year-old to stop smoking?" We said, "Well, one of the suggestions we have is stop smoking yourself." His response was, "Well, he's supposed to listen to me because I'm the parent."

Wouldn't raising children be so much simpler if that were true? You are the role model and the parent. You are the teacher and the role model. You show children not only through your words, but your actions. As a matter of fact, you cannot not communicate! Even when you are not saying anything, your actions and nonverbal communication precede you. And children are natural observers of all things adult!

In addition to smoking, other negative behaviors students may witness at home are:

- disrespectful language
- conflict (with no resolution)
- abusive behavior (both physical and emotional)
- waiting until the last moment to get things done
- sarcasm
- indifference
- favoritism

In schools, likely behaviors students may observe include:

- disrespectful language
- teachers talking to other teachers when no one is to be talking
- adults interrupting instruction with PA announcements
- adults referring to one another or other students using unkind terms
- sarcasm
- indifference
- favoritism

One of the things that we find very fascinating is that adults keep doing the same thing over and over and over again, even if it doesn't work. To us, that's very baffling. If you discipline a child by handing out the same punishment over and over and over again, and you're not getting the result that you want, then we think you should do something else.

We have a very simple philosophy in our approach. If something doesn't work, do something else. But does this sound familiar? A teacher is in her classroom teaching and she wants the students to move to another location. "It's time for our reading groups," she announces, and then there is a long pause. The teacher notices they are not moving at all. The teacher repeats, "Okay, kids, I said it's time to move. Now move immediately." And the children still don't respond to that.

Some teachers, believe it or not, will yell louder, saying the same thing, and nothing happens. If you keep screaming and yelling, and the students still don't move, it seems to us that you should change your strategy. What the teacher could have done was to hold up a sign saying, "Move quickly . . . now." It might work! Anything other than the same verbal strategy! (Note that the folks working with the little drummer boy solicited and tried different approaches until they found one that worked.)

ASKING QUESTIONS

Language is like the water in which a fish swims. It is so ubiquitous it goes unnoticed. However, we can accomplish a lot of what we set out to do if we simply monitor the nouns and verbs that flow out of our mouths. Stop and ask yourself, "Do I use more direct orders to assist children in changing their behaviors or do I pose questions?"

Teachers and parents who *tell* children what to do will sometimes get a behavior to stop for the moment. For example, if a child is about to run into the street, the parent will shout a command: "Stop! Don't run out into the street." That is appropriate for a short-term goal. However, if you want a child's long-term behavior to change, you must use what Eric Berne refers to as your "adult" voice. The adult voice is non-judgmental and often in question format.

The adult voice is the voice of respect. When using the adult voice, the voice of resolution, you are asking for information from the other person rather than judging or making assumptions about him or her.

The language of the adult voice sounds like this:

- What can you do to think in a positive way?
- How do you think this will change the situation?
- I think you are on the right track.
- I realize that this may be a drawback for now; however, things can improve in time.
- This is what you did [negative behavior]. What can you do differently next time?
- How does [this behavior] add to your success?
- What stops you from doing [the desired behavior]?
- What can you do right now to feel comfortable in this situation?

That said, *not* every question is a good question. We found that teachers and parents who really had difficulty in terms of discipline always asked a silly question. That question was, "What are you doing?" We believe a more useful question is, "What should you be doing?" When you say, "What should you be doing?" it changes things a little bit, flips the brain around, and a child can't answer it the same way.

In addition, a question is irresistible to the brain. When you ask someone a question, he or she *cannot not* answer. You are in complete control. Try this—if I ask you right now, "Can you think of your left big toe?" you did one of two things. Either you sensed your left big toe or you said no in your head. Your focus was on the question that I posed. You may not have answered aloud; the answer is just as often internal, which is just fine for behavioral change. (An example of using questions to appeal to curiosity: "What's inside the drum?")

MISBEHAVIOR

There are other reasons why children misbehave today. For example, kids misbehave because of lack of love, uncaring parents, peer pressure, drugs, poverty, low self-esteem, lack of social skills, and unclear rules of behavior.

There's a tremendous influence from the media, which is preoccupied with celebrities, overemphasizes violence, twists values, and presents senseless programming. Also, unclear parental expectations are a big reason why kids misbehave, as is a lack of parental supervision, which is even more devastating to children.

These are just some of the reasons why our children misbehave. We could blame the media, we could blame all of these things, but if we *really*, *really* want to help out-of-control children, what we need to do is to pull in the reins and think about what we're doing in terms of setting clear expectations, understanding motivation, and choosing the correct intentions for proper behavior. It helps to keep a sense of humor too. As a last thought, we can cross our fingers and hope for the best!

So where do we start? The next chapter deals with developing trust and rapport. Trust and rapport are the foundation for all good relationships.

Please take a moment to reflect:

What behaviors and attitutes are the children in your life observing?
What are those observations teaching them?
Is it possible that there are unintended lessons embedded within those
    observations?
What is your unique contribution to the development of your children?

Chapter Three

How Many Ways Do I Trust Thee?

"No significant learning occurs without a significant relationship."

—Dr. James Comer

Key Points:

- People like people who are like themselves.
- "Relationships are all there is" (Margaret Wheatley).
- Credibility is one-third rapport.
- Rapport is unconscious and can be tested.

Positive rapport is the basis of all good relationships. Period. Now, the reality is, many of us leave this most fundamental requirement for positive relationships up to chance. We do our best with what we know. This chapter is both informative and instructional in the actual conscious physicality of establishing trust and rapport with another person.

ESTABLISHING RAPPORT

Credibility requires rapport and trust. Without rapport and trust, motivation becomes almost impossible. Without trust and rapport, we can accomplish short-term goals with others through pure force of will; however, such accomplishments are usually short-lived. Without trust and rapport, people often become belligerent, rowdy, and oppositional. Some just shut down.

Even at this early point in the discussion, you probably have determined that everything contained on these pages is about establishing trust, rapport, and relationships. You're right! That is what the Passion for Compassion approach is all about. Choosing or creating the appropriate intervention is actually easy when you know your child or student well and have a positive relationship with that young person.

The good news is that rapport is testable in your experience. That's right! Simply read and practice the information in this chapter to acquire this skill of master communicators.

Rapport is something that we, as human beings, do naturally and, we may add, unconsciously. Think about a situation where you met someone and immediately liked him or her. The two of you clicked and there was ease to your communication. Now, think of another time when you met someone whom you immediately disliked . . . you couldn't wait to end the conversation and get away from that specific individual. That is unconscious rapport in action! The next section will show how you can consciously get into rapport with anyone in less than three minutes.

Before we describe the process of consciously creating physical rapport with another, please familiarize yourself with these other rapport-building suggestions.

Global rapport-building suggestions:

- Note the personality style of the other person. Use the information in chapter 4 to determine what he or she desires.
- As Stephen Covey says, "Seek first to understand, then to be understood."
- Match the other's rate of speech and his or her tonality, if possible.
- Assume for the moment what he or she is telling you is true.

CONNECTING WITH OTHERS
THROUGH BODY MIRRORING

Quick test: Either reach back into your memory or observe people the next time you are in a group. Notice how you can tell who is in rapport and who is not, simply by noticing the body positions and movements.

Without hearing the words or tone of the conversation, you will be able to determine through body matching or mismatching who is getting along and who is not.

How can you be sure that rapport is apparent if someone were observing you working with a child? One quick way to establish rapport (on an unconscious level) is through nonverbal communication like body mirroring or matching a person's breathing patterns. Our focus here will be body mirroring. To achieve rapport with an individual, you make yourself appear to be like him or her by becoming a mirror for his or her body postures. The term we use for this is pacing and leading.

When you pace someone, you do what he or she does; you follow his or her lead. Then, after a couple of minutes, when you sense you have made a connection, you move from pacing to leading. To do this, you make a great big move (shift your body, cross your legs, uncross your legs). If the other person follows, that's your signal that he or she is in rapport with you. If he or she does not follow your body movements (a crossing or uncrossing of the legs, say), you need to go back and pace (follow) him or her again for another minute or so and then test with a lead again.

Warning: Be careful not to mimic the other person. Don't follow the other's changes in body posture too soon. The other person will think you are mocking him or her. We encourage folks to practice first with family members or good friends. If, while practicing, the other person asks you why you are doing everything he or she is doing, use that as good feedback and slow down the pace of following body movements.

CONCRETE EXAMPLE OF RAPPORT

We will take you through the following example of establishing rapport in a seated position. Know that you can do this standing, running, and even lying down! Sitting is simply the easiest translation for a book.

Let's say that person B is consciously establishing rapport with person A:

1. Person B allows person A to take a seat.
2. B notices how A sits. A has very good posture, and her legs are crossed.

3. B takes her seat and assumes the same posture.
4. They begin their conversation. After several seconds, A shifts in her seat and uncrosses her legs.
5. B notices the body change, waits 20–25 seconds, and then, in the natural flow of conversation, shifts her position and uncrosses her legs. Their body postures now mirror one another again.
6. The conversation continues. A shifts again and recrosses her legs.
7. B takes note. She waits 20–25 seconds and then, at a natural point in the conversation, crosses her legs again.
8. How long does B pace (follow) A? B paces A for about two minutes. Let's say after two minutes, B senses she has rapport with A. (Heads nodding together or simply a kinesthetic feeling). B then makes a great big move (leading). Usually, within the next few seconds, A will come into the same position that B is in. However, if A so much as shifts her weight or moves her arm, that's it! B just tested rapport through her leading and A responded. On the other hand, if A remains frozen in her position, B goes back to pacing (following) A. After a minute B tests (makes a great big move) again and watches for A to follow her. This is the way she knows consciously that she has successfully established rapport. Now, they can begin the work at hand.

WHEN TO BREAK RAPPORT

As a consultant of change, there are times when you will need to break rapport (we refer to this as "breaking state"). In this instance, you mismatch the other person's body postures. This sends the unconscious message that it's time to go.

We share with you the following examples:

- It is time to move on. (Time for both of you is a valuable resource. Sometimes you have to call it a day before you reach a resolution.)
- Your brain is beginning to overload. (Sometimes you have to process the information that has already been gathered before you can gather more.)
- Either of you is starting to devolve into a negative state. You can't be resourceful if you are angry.

It is important to note here that when you are in rapport with someone, you can disagree with what he or she says and still be in rapport. Once rapport is established, you want to check it periodically, just like you would maintain any other relationship.

Now that you are aware of this phenomenon, which Frank Bernieri from the University of Oregon refers to as "natural mimicry," you can examine the relationships you are in currently and assess them for the quality of rapport therein.

In addition to establishing rapport, before you can diagnose or design and implement a successful intervention, you need to know the student on a level other than the behavioral level. The following chapter brings your attention to other criteria of which you need to be aware.

Please take a moment to reflect now:

How would getting into rapport with another assist you in becoming a good listener?

How does it feel to be listened to?

What advantages does the ability to listen give a consultant/change agent?

How can you be sure that rapport is apparent if someone were observing you working with a child?

Chapter Four

Treasure Hunt: Exploring the Child's Model of the World

"Grown-ups never understand anything for themselves, and it is tiresome for children to be always and forever explaining things to them."

—Antoine de Saint-Exupery (1900–1944),
The Little Prince, 1943

Key Points:

- Meet students in their models of the world.
- What motivates people?
- How is personality connected to student behavior and motivation?

STUDENTS' MODEL OF THE WORLD

Before you can do interventions with children, you need to meet them in their model of the world. Suggestion: Observe adults who are known for their extraordinary capability in motivating and leading children to more positive beliefs, values, and behaviors. We predict that you will notice an adult who is taking a genuine interest in getting to know what is important to the child (without judgment).

For example, if we were to ask you what you would wish for your students upon graduation, you would probably respond with values like long life, wisdom, love of learning, good health, loving family, and other such wishes. If you were to poll these same students, most likely you would learn that beauty, popularity, and money are what are important to them.

Now, as through the ages, there are generational differences. What is important to keep in mind as you look through the interventions is who, specifically, is the student you are seeking to help. Before you can design or implement a successful intervention, in addition to establishing rapport, you need to know the student at a level other than a behavioral one.

The following are questions we suggest you ask as you seek to know the child on many levels:

• What is the student's learning style?
• Is he or she more motivated by power, affiliation, or achievement?
• What does this student value?
• What is the personality style of this student?

PHENOMENOLOGICAL REFERENCE: LEARNING STYLES

Knowing the student's learning style will allow you to establish rapport on an even deeper level than body mirroring. While information is collected through all of our sensory systems, each of us has a tendency to process information and to initiate our behavioral feedback through our "primary" sensory system. We then are referred to as a visual, auditory, or kinesthetic learner. Knowing that each person has his or her own dominant sensory system can help us understand how each student perceives the real world differently. Listening to the words each student uses often and then aligning your language pattern with his or hers enhances understanding between two individuals.

For instance, if a student says, "I can't picture what you mean" (visual language), your response should be, "What do you need to clear up the picture?" (visual language), not, "How can I help you get a handle on this?" (kinesthetic).

You can increase your ability to significantly influence students by matching them in their model of the world through your choice of predicates. To be an effective communicator, you need to be able to do two things: Know your own preferred style and then practice using other ones. Increasing rapport and the quality of relationships began with the body mirroring, pacing, and leading learned in the previous chapter.

We now take the next step in the concept of building rapport on an unconscious level. To continue building trust, understanding, and cooperation, one needs to listen to, and match, key words and micrometaphors the other person uses.

An important skill for many aspects of communication, listening to someone's language patterns can allow you to discern which modality he or she primarily uses to represent the world in his or her thinking. With this knowledge, one can then match the other's language, thereby increasing rapport and understanding.

Use the words below to practice your own language flexibility. An exercise to assist your flexibility in language follows the list.

VISUAL	AUDITORY	KINESTHETIC	NON-SPECIFIC
picture	tune	touch	think
clear	note	handle	reflect
focus	accent	throw	decide
perspective	ring	finger	motivate
see	shout	shock	understand
flash	growl	stir	plan
bright	tone	strike	know
outlook	sing	impress	consider
speculate	sound	move	advise
glimpse	hear	hit	deliberate
preview	clear	grope	develop
shortsighted	say	impact	create
discern	scream	stroke	manage
distinguish	click	tap	repeat
illustrate	static	rub	anticipate
delineate	rattle	crash	indicate
paint	ask	smash	discover
cloud	chord	sharpen	prepare
clarify	amplify	tangible	believe
graphic	harmonize	crawl	ponder

Exercise: Flexibility in Language

Directions: Read each statement. Decide whether it is visual, auditory, or kinesthetic. For the match, write another sentence in the same modality that basically means the same thing. For the two translations, write sentences *in a different modality* that mean the same thing. The first one is done for you.

1. My future looks hazy.
   Match: (Example: Visual—My future appears unclear.)
   Translate: (Example: Auditory—My future sounds like a misplayed chord.)
   Translate: (Example: Kinesthetic—I am groping to get a handle on my future.)

Now you practice:

2. My friend walks all over me like I'm a doormat.
   Match:

   Translate:

   Translate:

3. I can imagine what she is like.
   Match:

   Translate:

   Translate:

4. Who can help me clear this up?
   Match:

   Translate

   Translate:

5. Sarah doesn't listen to me.
   Match:

   Translate:

   Translate:

6. Do you ever ponder what motivates him?
   Match:

   Translate:

   Translate:

7. Does this ring a bell with you?
   Match:

   Translate:

   Translate:

8. I keep stubbing my toe on unexpected obstacles.
   Match:

   Translate:

   Translate:

PHENOMENOLOGICAL REFERENCE: BASIC NEEDS OF CHILDREN; POWER, AFFILIATION, AND ACHIEVEMENT

All students have three basic needs: power, affiliation, and achievement.

Power is defined as having a sense of control over one's own destiny. Affiliation is the feeling of being connected to someone or a group. Achievement is having the feeling of successful completion. Importantly, the studies of children who have been extremely violent in a school setting indicate that two of these needs, power and affiliation, were missing.

Whereas all children have these three needs, the hierarchy of needs will differ between individuals. Some of your students value power above all others, while some get their power not from themselves, but from their affiliations. Continuing, some of the students with whom you work value achievement above power and affiliation. That doesn't mean their successes need to be celebrated with balloons falling from the ceiling; a simple verbal acknowledgment is great.

PHENOMENOLOGICAL REFERENCE: PERSONALITY

Finally, before an intervention can be considered or designed, the personality style of the student needs to be determined. As anyone who has lived or worked with children will tell you, different children respond in different ways. What gets one child's attention simply bores another. Some of our children are motivated by sticks and some by carrots. Personality is what makes us unique, yet predictable. For better or for worse, our core personality is a genetic legacy, hardwired since birth. Just as we inherit hair and eye color from our parents, we also inherit their personality traits.

Since personality is hard-wired, it makes sense to get to know your children/students (especially the ones who challenge you behaviorally) through some kind of personality assessment. There are many out there that you may be familiar with already. Feel free to use the personality system or assessment that you find most comfortable.

The system we use, the CLICK Personality Inventory, was created and copyrighted by Denise Hecht. We find this simple inventory to be accurate as well as powerful. We use four basic categories: director, influencer, stabilizer, and perfectionist.

Step 1: Identification

Identify the student's personality style using these traits.
Answers the question: "How would I describe the student?"

Style 1: Director

Things said by or about the student:

"They make things happen."
"Just give me the bottom line."

Focus:

"When?"

Behavioral tendencies:

- Future-oriented
- Goal-oriented
- Accepts challenges
- Excels at problem solving
- Likes immediate results

- Makes quick decisions
- Likes leading and taking control
- Direct
- Takes risks and is daring
- Sees the big picture

Learning Style:

Tends to be auditory

Style 2: Influencer

Things said by or about the student:

"He works best under pressure."
"Where's the party?"

Focus:

"Who?"

Behavioral tendencies:

- In the present
- People-oriented
- Optimistic
- Enthusiastic
- Motivational
- Good communicator
- Good counselor or coach
- Interactive
- Entertaining
- Flexible

Learning Style:

Tends to be visual

Style 3: Stabilizer

Things said by or about the student:

"You can count on me."
"We" (get power from the group)

Focus:

"What if?"

Behavioral tendencies:

- Considers past and future
- Consistent
- Patient
- Desires to help others
- Loyal
- Calms excited people
- Predictable
- Task-oriented
- Team player

Learning Style:

Tends to be kinesthetic

Style 4: Perfectionist

Things said by or about the student:

"The pursuit of excellence."
"Punches holes in things."

Focus:

"Why?"

Behavioral tendencies:

- Past, present, and future
- Cautious
- Analytical
- Attentive to details
- Diplomatic
- Checks for accuracy
- Critical thinker
- Uses systematic approach
- Rules are to be followed

Learning Style:

Processes information using visual, auditory, and kinesthetic modalities!

Now that you have identified the particular personality style of the student, the next step is to become familiar with the motivational factors specific to that style.

Step 2: Specific Motivational Factors

Remember—*the person with the most behavioral flexibility has the most control.* Attending to different people in ways that motivate them enables you to be more effective at eliciting positive behavior changes. This section answers the question, "What is it that this student desires?" Each personality style has specific desires and needs that, when satisfied, not only enhance effective behavioral management but play a large role in prevention.

Director

Give them:

- Power
- Prestige and authority
- Challenges
- Varied activities
- Opportunity for individual accomplishments

Influencer

Give them:

- Public recognition
- Freedom of expression
- Group activities
- Opportunity to verbalize
- Opportunity to affiliate with others.

Stabilizer

Give them:

- Appreciation
- Harmonious, predictable environment
- Identification with a group
- Credit for work accomplished or achieved

Perfectionist

Give them:

- Quality and excellence
- Clear and enforced rules
- Opportunity to express expertise
- Reserved atmosphere

Step 3: Red Flags

The lists above describe different personality types and can also act as a guide to determine how to give someone what he or she needs. How can you put this all together to not only know how to prevent some negative behaviors but also to raise awareness of "thin ice" behaviors specific to the personality types? Below you will find some of this thinking done for you.

Director

Directors like to take risks. They are daring, and they like the new and different (varied activities). These are simply behaviors. Whether a person's behaviors result in positive or negative outcomes is a choice the individual makes.

For instance, those who embody the director's behaviors and couple them with clear, strong goals are also known as entrepreneurial. Those same behaviors, without a goal, may result or manifest themselves as teenage pregnancy, drug or alcohol use, or even gang participation. When you know you have a director in your care, make sure he or she creates and works toward challenging goals. In chapter 8, "Getting There from Here," you will find many varied activities for setting goals.

In addition, directors who note that they are not getting what they need in terms of being leaders (control, prestige, authority) will try to hijack the group, often using a loud voice. Yes, their first impulse is to yell. How do you remain in control while giving the director the illusion that he or she is in control? Look to the section "Step 4: Simple Interventions," found on the following pages.

Influencer

Looking at the personality indicators for the influencer, you see someone who likes to charge his or her battery through relationship with others. The good news is that influencers are typically stress-resistant. That said, school can be a very stressful place and even influencers can yield to the pressure. If the influencers in your life begin to self-isolate, or begin to appear sloppy or unclean, *pay attention!* Withdrawn influencers are on a downward spiral, and they tend to bring others down with them. Be sure they are getting opportunities to verbalize and plenty of public recognition. Note: Public *recognition* is very different from *attention!* So often we hear that this or that child is craving attention. When we go into the classroom to observe, it isn't attention at all but recognition in front of peers that he or she is craving. Again, we refer you to the section on simple interventions.

Stabilizer

How could anyone with the list of traits listed under stabilizer drive us crazy? Always ready to help, organized and on task, they tend to be our pets, whether at home or at school! Actually, there are a few things of which we need to be aware when we have stabilizers in our homes and classrooms. First, stabilizers get their power from the group. They tend to speak using the pronoun *we*; very seldom will they use the pronoun *I*. They like to be in the background. Therefore, they seek to become part of a group. Now, there is nothing wrong with that. What you need to be cognizant of is their choice of group. If they don't make a connection with a "positive" group, they will make a connection with any group that will welcome them. We all know too well the kind of groups that troll for members that are loyal, consistent, and team players—the makings of a perfect gang member. In addition, stabilizers tend to be indecisive; therefore, please don't overwhelm them with a lot of different things to choose from or expect them to make a decision in a short amount of time. The authors were at a Starbucks once and a mother was trying to get her young stabilizer to make a choice from the bakery case. There was a line behind the young lad. She was feeling the pressure and doing a good job transferring it to him, so to speak. Finally, Tony leaned down and whispered in his ear, "Take the cookie." The boy looked at Tony with relief and told his mother he wanted the cookie! Decision

made. Finally, if there is a lot of disharmony in the stabilizer's environment or there are ever-constant changes, he or she can shut down, go internal, and become passive-aggressive. The stabilizer won't be disruptive and won't do a thing!

Perfectionist

Please have mercy on the perfectionists in your lives. It is not easy to
hold onself to the standards to which perfectionists hold themselves day
in and day out. Perfectionists tend to be sensitive and often feel they are
misunderstood. Yes, it's true—a perfectionist's peas and mashed pota-
toes *can't* touch each other on the plate! We always say, "Never argue
with perfectionists because they are right." This holds true unless there
is a perfectionist who is not getting what he or she needs. When a perfectionist isn't given a chance to contribute, or is in an environment that
doesn't follow rules consistently, he or she has a tendency to become
hypercritical and a know-it-all. A perfectionist can "Yeah, but," you into
the ground.

Step 4: Simple Interventions

What are some simple interventions using personality styles? Now that
you have identified the personality style of the student and recognize his
or her motivational needs, it is time to begin thinking along the lines of
personality-specific interventions.

Director

Because directors desire power, challenges, and goals, it is advisable to
put them through the New Behavior Generator process, found in chapter 10 on page 77. A way to get immediate results, the New Behavior
Generator is a positive approach to use with all the styles, and we have
found it to be of particular value when working with directors. In addition, how can you maintain control while appealing to the director's
need for power and control? This can be accomplished through the
savvy use of language. We refer you to a pattern we employ often when
motivating directors (whether young or old), The Illusion of Choice.
This is used to give the student the illusion that he or she has choice. In
reality you, the teacher, counselor, or parent, have already determined
the end result.

Some examples:

1. Whisper or talk quietly.
2. Do your homework before or after dinner; it's your choice.
3. Answer the questions aloud or on paper.

Influencer

Considering that influencers want affiliation, public recognition, and the opportunity to verbalize, try giving them ample opportunity to report to the class, be it as the "town crier" or as the "summarizer" at the conclusion of a lesson. Make a large, public deal out of their successes. These are also the students who really respond to your attendance at events unrelated to the classroom in which they are involved.

Stabilizer

Taking into consideration stabilizers' likes, group identification, appreciation, and predictable environment, make sure they are aware of any changes to their schedules well in advance and give good reasons for the changes. Give them time and individual appreciation for the small steps they are accomplishing. Also, stabilizers benefit from working with peers or mentors, as they tend to derive their power from a group.

Perfectionist

Using the perfectionist's desires for achievement, excellence, and enforced rules, an approach we have found to neutralize some of the misbehavior in the perfectionist student is to make sure that any group this particular student is in (be it academic, physical education, or playground) verbalizes the rules and procedures clearly and with detail, and then adheres to them. Give perfectionists an opportunity to express their expertise. Ask them for their opinion. Perfectionists usually wait for others to solicit their opinions; they won't simply volunteer them. However, they will ask a lot of questions. Assist them in learning how to establish rapport with others.

Digesting all that you have just become familiar with in terms of personalities, take a few minutes and note which personality matches the pleas below. Answers can be found on page 33.

POP QUIZ ON PERSONALITIES

Match the plea to the personality type: place a D, I, S, P next to the statement (answers on page 33).

1. Please help me slow downandnotrushthroughwhatIdo.
2. Please help me to stand up for my rights (if you don't mind my asking).
3. Please help me to finish everything I start.
4. Please help me to be a little less independent, but in my own way, of course.
5. Please help me to be more laid back and help me to do that *exactly* right.
6. Please help me follow our established procedures today. On second thought, I'll settle for a couple of minutes.
7. Please put an anchor on my arm next time they ask for volunteers.
8. Please help me to relax my focus on insignificant details, even though any of them may cause significant problems later. Begin this tomorrow at 8:31:04 a.m.

Learning about and treating students as individuals is respectful. So is holding high expectations for your students. After you identify the student's learning style, values, and personality, you are now ready to select an intervention that you think has a likelihood of appealing to the specific student. The onus is now on the student to make new choices. Remember the reference to you as a behavioral consultant? You are in charge of the process of consulting (establishing rapport, knowing the student's "map of the world" [phenomenological reference], choosing appropriate interventions for the desired outcomes, and integrating change through the whole person); *the student is in charge of doing the change work.* You will provide feedback to encourage movement toward more positive beliefs and also make revisions where necessary.

Now is a good time to integrate all that you have just learned. Think about how it applies to the specific children in your life. When you come back, chapter 5 will be waiting for you. Chapter 5 begins the journey of changing beliefs to change behavior. Curious? We thought you'd be . . . after your break, we'll meet you at chapter 5.

Reflecting upon the personality styles:

- What discoveries did you make about yourself?
- How can those discoveries assist you on your journey to becoming an extraordinary motivator of students?

Thinking of others' personality styles:

Please respond to the following statements:

- It's not the differences that divide us. It's our judgments about each other that do.
- "Being open and being attentive is more effective than being judgmental. This is because people naturally tend to be good and truthful when they are being received in a good and truthful manner." —John Heider

ANSWERS TO THE POP QUIZ ON PERSONALITIES

1. director or influencer
2. stabilizer
3. influencer
4. director
5. perfectionist
6. director
7. stabilizer
8. perfectionist

How did you do?

Chapter Five

Unleashing the Power of Beliefs

"What you see depends on what you thought before you looked."

—Eugene Tauman

Key Points:

- Beliefs drive behavior (neurological levels of learning and change).
- "You can't solve a problem on the same level on which it occurs" (Albert Einstein).
- Confusion precedes clarity.
- What's a meta for?

When working with students to improve behavior, oftentimes we do things simply because that is the way they have always been done. Take behavior modification, for instance. Most of us have invested a lot of time and energy into this approach, only to learn what those who have tried it before us have learned—simply, it rarely works! Einstein told us, "You can't solve a problem at the same level on which it occurs." Placing that idea in the behavioral arena moves us closer to where and how we must work with our children if we in fact want to assist these students in lasting, positive behavioral change.

We, as human beings, exist on many different levels of thinking and being. These neurological levels, developed by Robert Dilts, are expressed in the diagram below (Figure NL). In a sense, what the diagram illustrates is that we as human beings have a natural hierarchy involving experiences. When we change something at an upper level, let's say at the belief level, it automatically alters the levels below it; changing something on the lower level might but will not necessarily change the levels above it.

Figure NL: Neurological Levels of Learning and Change

* Identity—Who am I?
* Beliefs/Values—Why do I do it?
* Capabilities—How do I do it?
* Behavior—What do I do?
* Environment—Where, when, and with whom do I do it?

Looking more closely at the neurological levels, one could define:

Identity: the sense of self or how we see ourselves in the world, based on our beliefs, values, and actions.

Beliefs and values: literally give an individual permission or the motivation to use his or her capabilities.

Capabilities: the mental strategies or blueprints that direct behavior.

Behaviors: the specific and observable actions and behaviors of an individual.

Environment: the concrete context that affects behaviors and reactions of an individual.

To bring the neurological levels to a level of concreteness, the following statements show how limits or possibilities could come from any of the levels described. Following is the structure of an empowering belief.

Identity	"I am a creative person."
Belief	"Creating is easy and exciting for me."
Capability	"I have a creative way of doing things."
Behavior	"I can come up with three or four options for this problem."
Environment	"This classroom/home and my teacher/parents are conducive to creative problem solving."

The possible structure of a limiting belief:

Identity	"I am not a good student."
Belief	"I am not very smart."
Value	"I find school useless."
Capability	"I can't figure out how to study."
Behavior	"I failed many of my tests."
Environment	"I don't have any place to study."

As you look at the levels above, always keep in mind that beliefs are what drive behaviors. What one believes manifests itself directly through behavior. For instance, if a child believes he or she is a "good student," you will see that in his or her behaviors—cooperation and diligence even when the subject area is challenging to him or her. On the other hand, if a child believes that he or she is unintelligent, hyper, or lazy, the behaviors manifested could run the gamut from giving up easily to not even trying to being disruptive.

The good news/bad news about beliefs is that they are not about reality. We hold strongly onto our beliefs—environmental and behavioral evidence most likely won't change a belief—regardless of whether the belief is positive or limiting. The beliefs that are most influential are generally those that people are the least conscious of—like the water in which a fish swims.

Change must occur on the belief level to ensure long-term change on the behavioral level. When working with children who are struggling, we need to constantly reexamine our own beliefs, in regard to both the specific student and the system in which we find ourselves doing our work. Congruence or alignment of these levels is necessary for everything from effective communication to achieving goals.

Sit back and relax as we tell you a story to illustrate this point. A high school teacher in northern New Jersey told us this story about a sophomore in one of her classes:

This young man was a product of another tragic home situation. His father was physically abusive to his mother, so much so that they had sought refuge in a shelter for some time. When he entered her classroom, the family had been reunited and supposedly the father was keeping his hands to himself.

This young man's behavior in class was atrocious. While working on projects, he would smear glue on the desks. He was not permitted to use scissors, for he would threaten the other students, and he would hang from the windows. She knew that punishment was not going to help. The teacher did not refer him to the assistant principal, but to guidance, hopefully to get some much-needed help. Unfortunately, this didn't seem to work. Yet she kept trying and let this boy, through her rapport with him, know that she believed in him. One day, he hung around and told her he would like to share something with her. When she indicated her interest, he took a shopworn letter out of his pocket. From the creases she could tell it had been folded and refolded many times, indicative of how dearly it was valued. As she read the words in front of her, she realized it was a form letter some colleges send out to sophomores, simply an advertising ploy. However, she shared with him her excitement at the potential in front of them. She pointed out to him the "secret password" on the bottom that would allow him access to a website. He said he knew; he had gone onto the site and read what they had to say. So she asked, "What are you going to do?" He replied, "Well, you know I haven't earned very good grades in the past, but now I need to begin working." And from that point on he settled down in class and even did homework. The letter represented someone's belief in him, which altered his belief about himself, which drove the behaviors that heretofore had been buried.

METAPHORS

One of the methods we have found to be extremely useful in changing limiting beliefs is the use of metaphor, or "teaching tales." With the assistance of certain metaphors, we begin to extend the boundaries of beliefs about thinking and behavior.

As stated earlier, our students and we exist on many different levels of thinking and being. Oftentimes, the behaviors we are witnessing in our young folks are being driven by limiting beliefs that are completely out of the students' awareness. Much of what they are doing is unconscious. An interesting way to work on the unconscious level is through the use of metaphor. Sheldon Kapp, in his book *Guru: Metaphors from a Psychotherapist* (1971), defines metaphor as follows: "Generally, a metaphor is defined as a way of speaking in which one thing is expressed in terms of another, whereby this bringing together throws new light on the character of what is being described."

Whenever we explain an idea or concept by saying it's like something else, we are using metaphor. Metaphors can be anecdotes, jokes, parables, and stories that can guide or influence students' thinking and behavior. They can be effective in illustrating a point, motivating a student to do something, or even handling resistance. When metaphors are used properly, they can be elegant linguistic agents of change by providing a vicarious internal experience for the listener. Metaphors, like all good stories, work on an unconscious level and by nature are indirect forms of communication. Telling a metaphor is nonthreatening and taps into the student's imagination and inner resources.

Even a simple quote can be used to offer up a vicarious suggestion:

- "Failure is only the opportunity to begin again more intelligently." ——Henry Ford (This can be said to a student who is failing.)
- "Some men see things as they are and say, 'Why?' I dream of things that never were and say, 'Why not?'" —George Bernard Shaw (This might be said to a child who needs to feel empowered.)
- "Life is either a daring adventure or nothing." —Helen Keller (This could be said to a student who needs encouragement to act.)

When a student expresses some area of experience where he or she feels limited because of limiting beliefs, or perhaps sees no options at all, the telling of a metaphor (actual or experienced) may illustrate the experiences of another in overcoming a problem that is the same as the student's and suggests to the student, directly or indirectly, ways in which to deal with the experience. The metaphor, of course, has a resolution to the problem, which hopefully is integrated into the student's own situation.

The major requirement for an effective metaphor is that it meets the student in his or her model of the world. In other words, the metaphor must realistically relate to the relationships and patterns in the student's world, it must possess a structure equivalent to the problem situation, and the problem must have a solution. The metaphor should be structurally the equivalent of the student's problem and shed new light on the problem. The content of the metaphor doesn't necessarily have to be the same. If the content is too exact to the student's problem, the metaphor might be too obvious and lose its effectiveness because of that.

Metaphors, or "teaching tales" as we have called them, have the capacity to persuade individuals to change their limiting beliefs or behaviors instantly. Actually, teaching stories are an ancient tradition. Stories have always been a way to pass on traditional values, ethics, and morality. Movies and good books are longer forms of teaching tales. After you read a good book, for example, you feel transformed somehow, particularly if you have identified with one of the characters (hopefully the good guy or gal!).

Stories, as we have indicated, reach and teach people on many levels, both consciously and unconsciously, socially and psychologically. Stories have a way of indirectly affecting another without the threat of direct confrontation. Sometimes one is affected by the whole story, other times by a simple phrase.

Stories, in essence, are nonthreatening and engaging and can bypass normal resistance to change. Of course, in order for an individual to tell another a story, there must be trust and rapport between the parties and responsiveness to one another.

Stories bear repeating. They can not only affect limiting beliefs, but also have the ability to motivate, teach about relationships, create openings for students to talk, transmit values, and lastly, help students deal with all sorts of conflict, both inner and outer.

Before you go on to chapter 6 for additional interesting interventions, we leave you with one of our favorite teaching tales, taken from the book *Reframing* by Richard Bandler and John Grinder.

A very old Chinese Taoist story describes a farmer in a poor country village. His neighbors considered him very well-to-do. He owned a horse that he used for plowing and for transportation. One day his horse ran away. All his neighbors exclaimed how terrible this was, but the farmer simply said, "Maybe."

A few days later the horse returned and brought two wild horses with it. The neighbors all rejoiced at his good fortune, but the farmer just said, "Maybe." The next day the farmer's son tried to ride one of the wild horses. The horse threw him and the son broke his leg. The neighbors all offered their sympathy for his misfortune, but the farmer again said, "Maybe." The next week conscription officers came to the village to take young men for the army. They rejected the farmer's son because of his broken leg. When the neighbors told him how lucky he was, the farmer replied, "Maybe."

Obviously, this story shows how meaning operates as a function of context. It helps us appreciate the importance of context and how it can quickly shift the perception of events. When we change the context, we transform meaning.

Reflection questions:

When have you been most satisfied working with children?
What is it about working with children you find most satisfying?
What assumptions or beliefs are embedded in your replies to the questions above?
How do you invite fresh thinking into your deliberations?

Chapter Six

Reframe to Transform

"There is nothing either good or bad, but thinking makes it so."

—William Shakespeare

Key Points:

- Possibility is created with language.
- Words shape our beliefs and impact our actions.
- Ronald Reagan was a master reframer.

Reframing is an easy way to create desirable changes in students. In its simplest form, reframing can be used in general conversation to change the meaning of a statement or experience. By changing the meaning you redefine or relabel something by using a different word or set of words so that the statement or event means something else.

For example, if someone says, "I'm gullible" in a self-defeating way, you can respond as follows: "It's not that you are gullible, you just are open to new ideas, which keeps you from getting stuck in the past or from becoming stale." Again, if someone says, "The teacher said I was a slow student," the response can be, "It's not that you are slow, you just take your time to think things through."

Reframing is usually perfect for those who think negatively when they refer to themselves and others. Words shape our beliefs and impact our actions. Words like *lazy* or *hyper*, for example, tend to imbed limiting beliefs. Here is a list of words with their possible reframes:

driven	—no, energetic
stubborn	—no, determined
loud	—no, dramatic
sloppy	—no, creative
rebellious	—no, independent

Reframing can also be used to change the meaning of an event. For example, suppose a student fails a test, retakes the test, and fails it again. He or she may really view the whole event as personal failure. A simple reframe could go like this: "You know there is no such thing as failure, only feedback. Let's see what information or feedback we can gather about this test so we can take a different approach. We can also investigate how you take the test mentally. This may help the next time you have to take a test."

Reframing gives the word *failure* new meaning and can possibly help the student continue to work because of a different perspective about the word *failure*.

People get energized when different options or perspectives are presented to them. Changing the frame of an experience can have a major influence on how one perceives, interprets, and reacts to that experience. The purpose of reframing is to help students experience their actions and the impact of their beliefs from a different perspective and potentially be more resourceful or have more choice in how they react. Just as different picture frames can change the perception of what the picture represents, changing the frame of an experience or thought can alter or transform the meaning of that thought or event. Simply put, reframing opens up possibilities!

Read how reframing completely transformed the following events.

Political Spin

During the 1984 campaign, there was considerable concern about Ronald Reagan's age. Speaking during the presidential debate with Walter Mondale, Reagan said, "I will not make age an issue of this campaign. I am not going to exploit, for political purposes, my opponent's youth and inexperience." Reagan's age was not an issue for the remainder of the campaign!

Failure as Feedback

There is a story about Thomas Watson Sr., the first president of IBM. A young worker had made a mistake that lost IBM one million dollars in business. She was called in to the president's office, and as she walked in, she said, "Well, I guess you have called me here to fire me." "Fire you?" Mr. Watson replied, "I just spent one million on your education!"

Context Reframe

A father brought his headstrong daughter to see Milton Erickson, the famous hypnotherapist. He said to Erickson, "My daughter doesn't listen to me or her mother. She is always expressing her own opinion." After the father finished describing his daughter's problem, Erickson replied, "Now isn't it good that she will be able to stand on her own two feet when she is ready to leave home?" The father sat in stunned silence. That was the extent of the therapy—the father now saw his daughter's behavior as a useful resource for her later in life.

We invite you to try your hand at reframing in the exercise below:

EXERCISE IN REFRAMING

Person A makes a statement about another person, implying something negative. Person B changes the negative word through reframing the meaning. Or, you may set up "two people" in your mind to carry out this exercise.

Example:
Person A: "She is stingy."
Person B: "It's not that she's stingy; she is thrifty."

Some words to try:

choosy	overemotional
irresponsible	gullible
indiscreet	grim
impulsive	handicapped
rigid	hyper
weak	noisy

CLASSROOM APPLICATIONS

Either by yourself or with a colleague, challenge or reframe the following statements overheard in a faculty lunchroom.

"That kid is a monster. He's absolutely impossible."
"If I find five punctuation errors in a composition, he will earn zero points, an F."
"I'm going to keep him in from recess until he completes his science homework."
"This child is learning disabled."

Reflection:

What do you think of a child who constantly says, "I don't know" or "I don't understand"?
Some folks think that these words indicate that the child has a strong desire to learn. What do you think would happen if you replied to a student who starts every sentence with "I don't know" with "That lets me know you are the kind of student who really wants to learn"?
What words, statements, or questions can you use with your students to generate hope or new possibilities or increase focus on positive solutions?
Where does your potential lie?

Chapter Seven

School Talk:
Work Hard, Be Smart, Do Well

"How we spend our days is, of course, how we spend our lives."

— Annie Dillard

Key Points:

- Work hard, do well, be smart.
- Shape behavior instead of modifying behavior.
- Praise effort, not intelligence.
- Focus on self-control, not self-esteem.

The Passion for Compassion approach encourages teachers and parents to be conscious of their language. In the previous chapter, we examined reframing, a way to use your language to assist others in letting go of beliefs and perceptions that could limit possibilities. In this chapter, we will examine language again. This time we will focus on the message and the resulting behaviors that it shapes.

Language is the most abundant, free resource within your control. The language you choose can make a significant difference in shaping young peoples' behaviors. Additionally, Steven Pinker refers to language as the "stuff of thought." Assuming this is true, the question becomes, "What 'stuff' is feeding your students' thoughts and therefore their resulting behaviors?"

Let us take a moment and conceptualize language through a food metaphor. We are aware that there are "healthy" food groups. These are the foods we should eat most often—they nourish our bodies and help us maintain a state of good health and even peak performance.

Then there are the not-so-healthy foods, like fats and sweets—let's say candies, for instance. Candy is deliciously satisfying every now and again. However, if we were to dine on it regularly, we could fall prone to any number of conditions that would seriously compromise our performance.

Looking at the craft of education, language is the food we use to give form to others' behaviors. Can you be certain that you are dishing out healthy food rather than sugarcoated milk chocolate?

Please take a moment and ask yourself:

How do I praise my students' successes?
What do I say to them, specifically?
How invested am I in building high self-esteem in my students?

Your answers to the above questions are indicative of two things. The first confection we will sample from the bag of sugarcoated milk chocolate is self-esteem.

After nearly two decades of teachers, parents, and therapists focusing their efforts on boosting children's self-esteem, Roy Baumeister of Florida State University and a team of psychologists he has led have found no evidence that boosting self-esteem through school programs or therapeutic interventions leads to any positive outcomes.

Contrary to the enthusiastic claims of the self-esteem movement, the effects of self-esteem are small, limited, and not all good. Baumeister claims, "High self-esteem folks are more likely to be obnoxious, to interrupt, and to talk at people rather than with them. My conclusion is that self-control is worth 10 times as much as self-esteem." Even more alarming, Heatherton and Vohs (2000) state, "A youth who develops a big ego, which then gets threatened or deflated by social rejection, is potentially dangerous."

A classroom teacher knows this all too well. Who would you rather have at a desk in front of you: a student who is sure that she or he knows everything about the lesson you are teaching or a student who is not completely sure she or he knows everything? The latter student tends to pay more attention, whereas the former student feels he or she "knows it all" and can ignore what you are saying.

We are not saying don't let a child know she or he is doing well. However, we do advocate for a certain way of phrasing things when giving children feedback, which we will share with you at the conclusion of this chapter.

In addition, as you familiarize yourself with the interventions located within this book, you will notice that many of them take a brain-based approach to assist in the students' acquisition of self-control. And, as Baumeister states above, "Self-control is worth ten times as much as self-esteem."

The second reach we take into our bag of chocolates brings out the yummy temptation to praise children for their "natural" talents, whether that talent is in the classroom (IQ), on the playground (EQ), or on the court (AQ—athletic quotient). One often hears adults, be they parents or teachers, say things like, "Oh! You've really got a head for math!" or "Wow! What a gift you have for writing!"

Carol Dweck in her recent book *Mindset* warns that praising children's intelligence harms their motivation as well as their performance. She, like us, advocates for the message that clearly states that skills and achievement come about through commitment and effort, *not* talent alone.

In her book, Dweck describes two different mind-sets that folks can have, fixed or growth. Students and adults with a fixed mind-set tend to believe that talents and abilities are an either/or game . . . either you have them or you don't. Growth mind-set folks know that talents can be developed—that the mind and body can, with effort, improve over time.

As stated in chapter 5, beliefs drive behavior. These two distinct mind-sets reflect differing beliefs that result in two radically different behavioral sets. Fixed mind-set students, who have been told over and over that their talents are innate, tend to try to prove themselves over and over again, maintaining their "smart" identity at all costs, sometimes even cheating.

For fixed mind-set people, it's a black-and-white world—you are either smart or dumb. This limits their ability to take a risk. Those who try new approaches might fail and therefore expose themselves as not having the brilliance that they have been told they have. They often suffer anxiety over disapproval of their ideas. Operating from a fixed mind-set can cause an 8-year-old to lie about a score or the CEO of Enron to be above listening to the voices of warning. "Nothing ventured, nothing lost" sums up their philosophy.

Growth mind-set people, on the other hand, act from the idea that success comes from learning, not proving that they are smart. Their guiding axiom is "Nothing ventured, nothing gained." They tend to embrace challenges.

Dweck says, "When students succeed, teachers should praise their efforts or their strategies, not their intelligence. (Contrary to popular opinion, praising intelligence backfires by making students overly concerned with how smart they are and overly vulnerable to failure.)"

When students fail, teachers should also give feedback about effort or strategies—what the student did wrong and what he or she could do now. The Passion for Compassion approach teaches children that there is no such thing as failure, only feedback, and that feedback is simply information that can be incorporated into the way children do things or not. In matters of schoolwork, we say it is only a mistake if you don't learn from it. We feel that this is a key ingredient in creating mastery-oriented students. *You are only as good as your feedback!*

In other words, teachers should help students value effort. Too many students think effort is only for the inept. Yet sustained effort over time is the key to outstanding achievement.

At back-to-school night last year, an Advanced Placement calculus teacher announced that doing well in a challenging math course such as his is not about intelligence, but rather about patience. He claimed that, "Those who keep struggling eventually discover the solution. So, parents, ask yourselves—how much patience does your son or daughter have?" We felt that was some of the best information we had ever received at a school function!

Next, we move on to goal setting in chapter 8 and concrete interventions in the subsequent chapters. However, before we make that shift, we would like to take some time to sum up the power of language. Please read and think about the following true story, an example of using language to appeal to a student's strengths and to create a double bind. This story comes from one of the authors' real-life experiences.

Halloween is big in our home. We decorate in September. Ghosts in the trees; scary things coming out of the ground; pumpkins, hay, and flowers. We have always made it a family affair.

When my children were still young, we had new neighbors move in next door. Their oldest son, Jack, was a bit of a troublemaker. That Halloween, after many years of undisturbed decorations, many of our treasures were trashed. To this day, we don't know who did it, but I made my assumptions, just as you would. What did I do?

I visited the neighbors and asked to speak with Jack. I told him what happened to our decorations and then asked him to help keep my home safe. I told him how I had noticed that even though he was new, others in the neighborhood looked up to him and followed him. I told him I valued his ability to send a message that the others would respect. I asked him to use his talents to stop the others from destroying my children's decorations.

The bad news is, after graduating high school, Jack got in trouble with the law. The good news is, my decorations have never been tampered with again.

Please take a moment and play with these questions:

What, in how I framed my language, do you think worked in my favor?
What seed could you plant today that could make the most difference in the future of a student?
How will you monitor your language and its content?

Chapter Eight

Getting There from Here

"Sometimes a circle feels like a direction."

—Louise Goffin

Key Points:

- Goal setting
- Planning to control impulsivity
- Vision to action

To begin this chapter on goal setting, we want to share a story with you that we believe illustrates the ideal relationship between student and adult, because both partners in the collaborative relationship (teacher-student, parent-child, counselor-child/young adult) need to have a goal in mind when entering into a helping relationship.

This story is about Milton Erickson (mentioned previously), a brilliant psychiatrist who was voted one of the ten most influential therapists by the readers of *Psychotherapy Networker* in March/April 2007. Erickson's ability to help folks move from severely limiting behaviors to more positive behaviors led him to be viewed as a "therapeutic wizard."

Dr. Erickson was raised on a farm in Missouri. One sunny summer day, when Milton was about 11 years old, a horse from a neighboring farm ran into the field where Milton was working. He saw the horse and knew it didn't belong there, so he hopped up on its back and rode it back to its home farm, about six miles down the road. A surprised farmer watched as Erickson rode the escaped horse up to its barn. The farmer hailed Erickson and said, "That's my horse."

"Yes sir, I know," replied the young Erickson.

"How did you know it was my horse and how did you know it belonged here?" the surprised farmer inquired.

"That was easy," replied Milton. "The horse knew where to go. I just kept his head straight and if he tried to veer off into a pasture, I refocused him on the road in front of him."

That is how Dr. Erickson worked with people. When people sought him out for help, he believed that they had the resources they needed to overcome the psychological limitations they were facing. He simply asked questions to keep them focused on what would be beneficial for them.

So, now that you know your goal, we will explore some of the research on planning and goal setting to underscore how important this oft-overlooked step in long-term behavioral change is.

GOAL SETTING FOR STUDENTS

One good reason to teach goal setting to students is that goal setting moves them in a positive direction. It focuses their energy; it motivates them toward desired outcomes. Goals are what we want. Teachers can help students identify what they deem worthwhile and pertinent in order to custom-design their futures.

Thinking of your more challenging students provides another important reason to work actively on planning and goal setting. Let's look at the work of Reuven Feuerstein. He states that a child's cognitive abilities are developed unconsciously through the cultural stimuli passed on by his or her parents and grandparents. If these parents and grandparents are very centered in the present (sometimes for survival reasons), the child is not exposed to planning for and thinking about the future. This inability to plan manifests itself in the following progression, as described in Ruby Payne's *A Framework for Understanding Poverty*.

> If an individual has not developed the ability to plan, he or she cannot predict.

If an individual cannot predict, he or she cannot identify cause and effect.

If an individual cannot identify cause and effect, he or she cannot identify consequence.

If an individual cannot identify consequence, he or she cannot control impulsivity.

If an individual cannot control impulsivity, he or she has an inclination toward criminal behavior.

In addition, brain research indicates that what gets noticed by the mind is closely correlated with the goals of the person. In other words, your mind does what you tell it to do.

TOOLS AND EXERCISES

We call one of our favorite processes the Zander Letter. This is adapted from the book by Ben and Rosamund Zander, *The Art of Possibility*. Starting with the successful end in mind, at the beginning of the school year we ask students to write letters to someone who is dear to them. These letters are dated the last day of school. In these letters, they will tell their dear friends about the A they received in class. We instruct them to tell, in as much detail as they can, the story of how they achieved this extraordinary grade and what kind of person they have become because of this. We have done this with adults as well. The letters are gems! Not only that, the experience of writing them adds to the process of planning, which enables individuals to control impulsivity!

Teaching Strategic Thinking through Goal Setting

The three-phase model described in figure 8.1 can be used to assist children in thinking through what it takes to set a goal and devise an action plan. It is comprised of a present state, plan of action, and a desired state.

The desired state is the outcome. The plan of action is a step-by-step process to achieve the desired state. The plan of action may also be thought of as a series of short-term goals that lead directly to the major outcome.

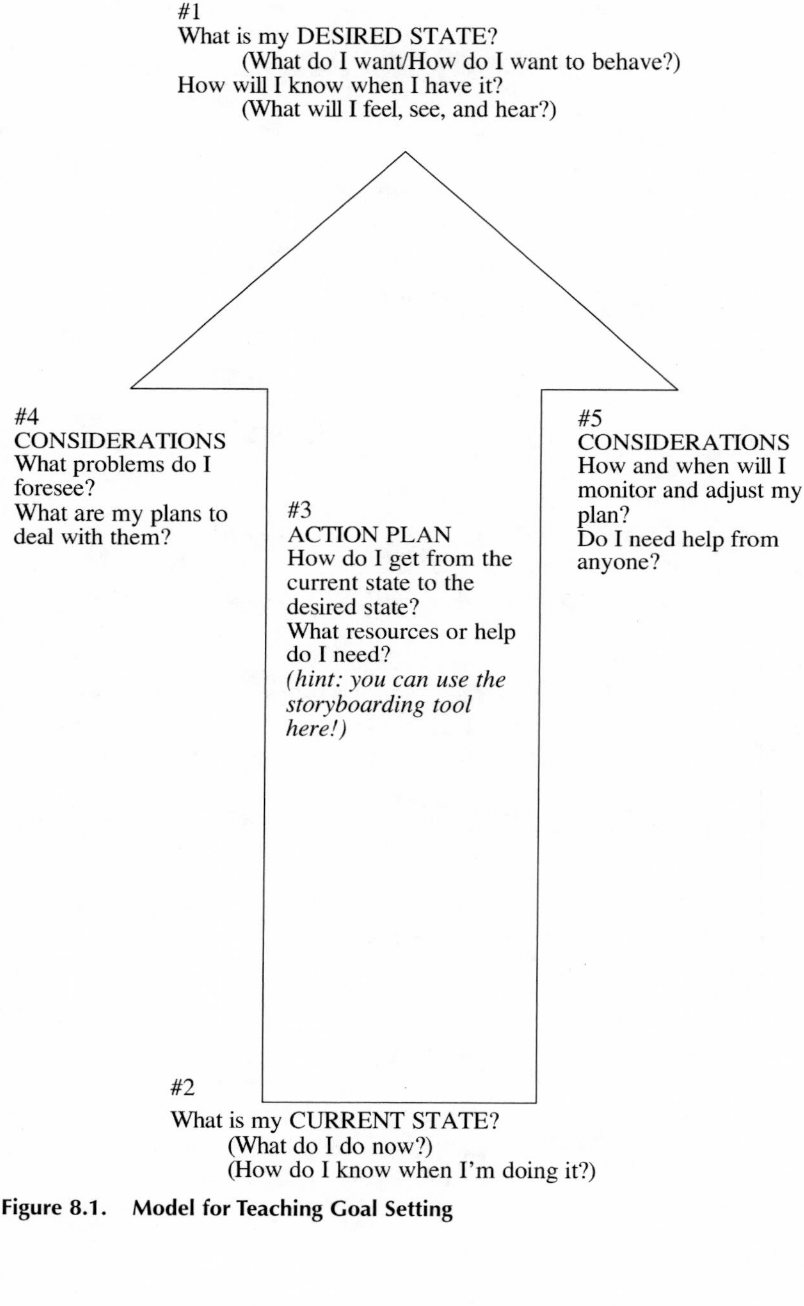

#1
What is my DESIRED STATE?
　　(What do I want/How do I want to behave?)
How will I know when I have it?
　　(What will I feel, see, and hear?)

#4
CONSIDERATIONS
What problems do I
foresee?
What are my plans to
deal with them?

#3
ACTION PLAN
How do I get from the
current state to the
desired state?
What resources or help
do I need?
*(hint: you can use the
storyboarding tool
here!)*

#5
CONSIDERATIONS
How and when will I
monitor and adjust my
plan?
Do I need help from
anyone?

#2
What is my CURRENT STATE?
　　(What do I do now?)
　　(How do I know when I'm doing it?)

Figure 8.1.　Model for Teaching Goal Setting

WELL-FORMED OUTCOMES

When setting goals with students, there are a number of safeguards that will almost guarantee an orderly and systematic plan for success. This "guarantee" is accomplished by asking some key questions at the onset of the process. The following key questions will help in formulating well-defined and well-formed goals and outcomes.

1. What do you want to achieve (rather than what don't you want or what do you want to avoid)? State this in the positive. For example, many students will tell you what they don't want ("I don't want to fail the test" or "I don't want to be overweight") as opposed to what they do want ("I want to pass the test successfully," "I want to be 120 pounds," or "I want to eat in a healthy way").
2. Can you describe the outcome with specificity? "I want to eat in a healthy way" is a good, positively stated goal; however, it is not specific enough. "I want to eat cereal, juice, and fruit for breakfast. I want a salad for lunch and fish for dinner." That goal is more specific and more concrete. Students should be able to tell you what they will see, hear, and feel when they have achieved their desired states.
3. How will you know when you have achieved this goal or outcome? How will you check along the way (benchmarks or a time line)?
4. What resources will you need (books, peer assistance, money, information, confidence, etc.)?
5. What do you have already that can help you?
6. What will this cost in time, money, or opportunity?
7. How will you test or evaluate your success?
8. How will you know when you have reached your outcome?
9. What are the consequences for others, for example, at home, school, or work?
10. Is this within your control? You can only achieve what you can control!

Students like to set goals about education, health, money, careers, leisure activities, family matters, and sports. Having them write goals and outcomes will, in most cases, give them better than an 80 percent chance of achieving the goals or outcomes. Or put another way, according to reliable research on the topic, individuals who don't clearly spell out and define their goals rarely reach them. Short-term goals are easier to achieve than long-term ones. For this reason, we highly recommended starting with one or two short-term and easily achievable goals.

Young people also like going for things that are worthwhile and real and important to them. Ask them what in their lives matters or what would be an important pursuit. Try to get students to go after something they really value, a core value of theirs. One way to get at the core values of students is to ask them first what they want through the key questions. When that is firm and specific in your mind, ask next, "What will that get you?" That will lead to a value of some kind. Ask next, "When you get that value, what will that get for you?" That should yield another value. Just continue asking the same question ("What will that get you?") until you come to a core value. You can identify a core value when the student repeats the same word or words during the questioning or when he personally identifies with the work.

An example of this process is as follows:

Teacher: What do you want?
Student: I want to be more outgoing.
Teacher: What will that get you?
Student: It will make me confident.
Teacher: And when you are confident, what will that do for you?
Student: It will make me feel proud.
Teacher: And what will that get you?
Student: It will make me feel that I am mature!

The core value here is growth as a person. Growth can be the motivating force for this individual in this case and in other matters related to this student's goals and future plans.

Lastly, a recommendation for working with goals is to *start with the end in mind*. Most people begin the goal-setting process from the present state, but if one starts from the desired state and works backward to the present state, there is a greater degree of certainty. For some, looking from the present to the future causes frustration because they immediately feel the goal is too far away and not achievable. Educators are very familiar with end-to-the-beginning planning.

STORYBOARDING

Storyboarding is essentially a great way to teach students goal setting and planning. Planning and goal setting are directly related to improved behavior and self-control. See tables 8.1 and 8.2 for two examples of storyboarding.

Storyboarding is an effective way to create the action plan needed to get from the current state to the desired state (outcome). With storyboarding, the student can begin to visualize the steps for achieving a goal. The process is simple. The student draws a minimum of five boxes. In box one, the student draws or writes the current state. In box five (or the last box), the student writes or draws the outcome/goal/desired state. Box number two then represents the first step, box three the second step, and so on. After the student masters five boxes, he or she can be expected to use this procedure for more elaborate goals with a greater number of steps. The student can be told that this is the procedure Hollywood uses to "map" out a film.

Table 8.1. Storyboarding: Example One

Storyboarding: Student may write or draw within the boxes. Student may record this in his or her journal. Another alternative is to post a large piece of paper on the wall and brainstorm the steps on there (just like Hollywood!).

Current State	Step 1	Step 2	Step 3	Goal/ Outcome/ Desired State

Table 8.2. Storyboarding: Example Two

Current State	Step 1	Step 2	Step 3	Step 4	Step 5	Goal/ Outcome/ Desired State

Chapter Nine

All Things Change When We Do

"Self-control is worth ten times as much as self-esteem."

—R. Baumeister (1996)

Key Points:

- The questions you ask direct your focus.
- See, hear, and feel your future.
- Young people have all the resources they need to effect change in themselves.
- Persistence, mastery, and effort are keys to success.

According to the Search Institute, children who know how to create and maintain resourceful states (persistence, flexibility, patience) tend to perform well both behaviorally and academically. Through their research, the Search Institute has determined that having a positive mental attitude, which is being able to see the good in any situation, is the first step toward success and a critical step in overcoming adversity.

How can you work with the children who are unable to access their resourceful states? Chapter 6 contained several ways to assist children in developing resources through the reframing of language. Chapter 7 addressed the idea of building in self-control and diligence.

In this chapter, several interventions are introduced that, when used by a caring consultant, can transform the lives of children and adolescents.

One way is to encourage them to ask themselves good questions internally (when they talk to themselves). Negative self-talk can lead an individual to feeling depressed, stressed, and anxious. Positive self-talk can lead to peak performance! In other words, questions direct your focus—the way you think and the way you feel.

Tony Robbins, a master motivator, tells us "a genuine quality of life comes from consistently asking quality questions." He adds, "Questions immediately change what we're focusing on and therefore how we feel." If you say, "Why aren't I popular?" you will constantly focus on all the reasons you think you're not. If you say, "How can I look for opportunities to get more popular?" you tend to seek out opportunities. Again, if a student says, "Why do I always fail?" the answer might be something like, "Because I'm not intelligent or because I lack talent." If, on the other hand, the student says, "What are the steps I can take to be successful?" the student will focus in a more positive direction.

Examining questions students ask themselves and helping them to ask good questions will lead them to superior states of mind. One good question to add to their arsenal of questions is, "How can I turn this around?"

Next, we use a shift in perspective to assist students in increasing their self-control.

SWITCHING PERSPECTIVES

When a person views something from a particular perspective, it's called a point of view. The ability to view something from different perspectives has great value.

Associated

Viewing from an associated perspective means seeing something from your own eyes, looking out from your eyes onto what you are viewing. Picture yourself in the first car of a roller-coaster train. Looking around you, you see the safety bar in front of you, you notice the tracks going upward, and you also see the people on the side waiting to go on the next ride.

As the train begins to move, you notice now only the tracks and the sky as it moves to the top of the track high above. You hear the iron

noises of the wheels against the tracks and you begin to feel the antici-
pation of the drop that's going to occur shortly when the roller-coaster
train hurtles downward. That is being associated into the experience.
You see, hear, and feel the experience.

Disassociated

Viewing the same incident above from a disassociated point of view
means to see it as if you were watching it on a big movie screen from a
slight distance. You see the same roller coaster, the train, and the train
moving upward, but somehow because of the distance of "watching you
over there," the feelings are not as powerful or intense.

By disassociating from unpleasant feelings, you can remain resourceful and creative and are more able to deal with difficult situations.
Learning to associate and disassociate gives you an upper hand in
everyday living. Below is a way to practice how to associate and disassociate at will. Of course, if you want to increase pleasant feelings,
memories, and thoughts, you naturally associate into the memory or image. If you want to neutralize or even reverse negative feelings, memories, and thoughts, you disassociate from the experience.

EXERCISE ON DISASSOCIATION AND ASSOCIATION

Association

Have the student think (with eyes closed) of any pleasant memory, and
have the student associate into it totally. Make sure he is looking at the
experience from his own eyes, seeing, hearing, and feeling the experience fully.

Next, tell the student to make the image(s) a little bigger and
brighter and in color so that the feelings of pleasantness increase as
well. He can also make the sounds or words, if there are any, more
pleasant-sounding.

Lastly, have the student try to associate into several other pleasant
memories. Have the student choose a few from different contexts—
school, work, home, and so on. For each one, tell the student to pretend
that he or she really is in the experience fully, as if it were occurring in
the moment.

DISASSOCIATION

Think of a mildly unpleasant experience and have the student view the experience as if he or she were viewing it on a movie screen. Tell the student to see everything that is in the experience, but to make the memory appear in black-and-white and perhaps a bit dimmer.

At the same time, have the student view the memory from an interested observer point of view. He is watching, but is detached from the memory.

Have the student choose a few other unpleasant or negative experiences and follow the same procedure. Having the student practice being an observer of his own experiences enables him to generalize disassociation to other negative situations.

The following are a few more strategies for creating and maintaining positive states for peak performance, both academically and behaviorally. Each one may help students perform in a congruent fashion.

THE MIND-PICTURE INTERVENTION

The following exercise using visual patterns is especially useful for changing students' feelings and motivating them to become engaged in activities they presently don't enjoy, like doing homework, working in groups, or even participating more in class. It takes about twenty-five minutes to do properly.

1. Tell the student to picture in his mind something he really likes to do with passion, something he is wildly compelled to do with passion. He should see this through his own eyes (associated).
2. Next, get a picture of something he needs to do (the task), so he might as well enjoy it. This picture should be disassociated or seen as if watching it on a large television or movie screen.
3. Tell the student to hold picture two in his mind, with picture one right behind it. (You may have to guide the student through this, so take your time.) Tell the student to quickly open up a small hole in the center of picture two, so he can see picture one through the small hole. Then tell the student to make the hole as big as he can to see picture one and feel the positive feeling associated with picture one.

4. Lastly, tell him to shrink the hole down quickly, but only as quickly or fast as he can to help retain the feeling that picture one causes.
5. Repeat this process at least five times. What you want to do is attach the feelings of picture one to picture two (the task).

Note: This activity is effective as a whole class activity as well.

GETTING STUDENTS "UNSTUCK"

Very often, disaffected students feel stuck in their school experience. By stuck, we mean unmotivated, unfeeling, or disinterested in school, schoolwork, or even extracurricular opportunities. The following exercise helps students get unstuck (and stay unstuck).

First, it helps to know that these students are deeply immersed in their internal feelings (stuck state). The idea is to get them out of their internal state of mind to an external state. In order for this to happen, students need to understand the difference between an associated state and a disassociated state.

You can explain this by giving the following example. Have them picture an experience first in their minds (associated state). Next, have them visualize the image of the experience on the wall away from them (disassociated state). Ask them how pushing it (the picture) away and seeing it on the wall affects their feelings, if at all. Then have them bring the image back to their minds. Does it change their feelings? Usually, the associated feelings are stronger, more intense, or more real. Pushing pictures away in one's mind usually decreases feelings.

If the student or students are not visual, ask them to feel themselves float outside their bodies and look back at themselves sitting down. Ask them to pretend they are sitting across the room in different chairs. Can they get a sense of themselves across the room? Another way to get students to decrease or eliminate stuck states is to ask them to think of something that gets them down or slightly depressed.

Change their posture by telling them to look up with their hands over their heads and think of the incidents that get them down. They will definitely feel different (less intense or less negative), because this posture keeps one visual. Hands up and eyes up are powerful positions to "pop" individuals out of negative states.

Once the student has successfully felt the difference between being associated as opposed to disassociated, you can begin the exercise below. This exercise is one useful safeguard for getting someone unstuck.

Getting Unstuck Exercise

Usually, when a person is stuck, he is stuck in bad feelings. Having the person disassociate from these feelings (literally leaving the feelings behind or someplace else) will put him or her in a much better state of mind.
Exercise

1. Say to the student, "Imagine you are in a movie theater and you see a picture of yourself as you appear here, up on the screen" (point to the imagined screen so the student looks up and away).
2. When the student can fully imagine himself on the screen, ask the student to say yes or give a signal that he is there.
3. When the student signals or says yes, slightly touch the student on the shoulder to anchor the disassociated state. Discuss that you will touch the student before the exercise and that the touch sort of reminds the student to "be on the screen" disassociated from where he is sitting.
4. After the anchor has been established, you can repeat step three two or three times to make sure the anchor is firm.
5. Next, have the student briefly turn his head left or right. This is called a breaker state. Keep the head turned two or three seconds. Then return to a normal position straight ahead.
6. Elicit the stuck state next by saying, "Imagine or think of a time when you get stuck or feel stuck" (this should have been discussed prior to the exercise).
7. As soon as the student feels he has accessed the stuck state, again by thinking of it and giving you a signal, fire off the anchor of the disassociated state by touching his shoulder again.
8. The student will feel neutral at this point rather than stuck. Briefly point out that he should feel differently, not stuck.
9. Repeat this procedure if the student reports still feeling negative or stuck.

From this point, have the student go into the future and think now of when he used to feel unemotional or disinterested and ask how he feels now. The report should be neutral or slightly positive.

PERSONAL RESOURCES

Many struggling students lack the personal, internal resources to achieve a stated outcome. Examples of internal resources could include:

flexibility	happiness
confidence	persistence
decisiveness	helpfulness
caring	compassion
humor	organization

In some cases, students may not be able to identify resources or they may label the resource a different name. In any event, students must be able to access these resources in order to complete tasks and accomplish their stated goals. A simple way to activate these resources is through a number of questioning techniques.

Questioning to Bring Forth Resources

"As if" questions

Ask students to select a resource and act "as if" their outcome already has been achieved. So, for example, if a student states that she would like to behave more lovingly toward her brother, tell her to pretend that she is already acting in a loving way toward her brother.

Then suggest to the student that it is now six months from today's date. Ask the student to describe how she is acting. The student gives a description. "Now, what was the first step you took to get there? The second? The third?" The student has now outlined a step-by-step procedure to achieve the goal of "being loving." The student can now follow the plan to completion.

Modeling Another

A second way to get students to bring forth resources is to ask them if they know someone who is flexible, joyful, organized, and so on. Then ask them to picture in their minds this someone performing with the resource. Next ask them to pretend they are that someone by stepping into the person's body. Then say to them, "Now that you are the other person, imagine the person doing X in movie form." Tell them to describe what they are seeing, hearing, and doing. They can carry the image into the future.

Sometimes students will say they don't know anyone who displays the resource they seek, so imagination comes in handy here. Do the same as above, simply having the student imagine someone doing X and take it from there. Say to him or her, "OK, if you don't know anyone who is loving, imagine how someone would act if they were loving and describe that."

BRAIN MAPPING RESOURCES

Brain mapping involves the re-creation of personal resources through sensory information (visual, auditory, and kinesthetic senses). Each sensory modality above is mapped and checked internally and externally. Each time a check is made, the student gently presses or squeezes his finger or wrist to install the feelings of the resources.

Procedure for Brain Mapping

1. Select a time when you felt really good or resourceful.
2. Remember what you saw at that time (visual/external).
3. Recall any images you had at that time (visual/internal).
4. Remember any voices or sounds at that time (auditory/external).
5. Remember anything you said to yourself (auditory/internal).
6. Remember any sensations you had, like the wind blowing on your skin, someone touching you, and so on (kinesthetic/external).
7. Recall any internal feelings, such as happiness, competence, or compassion (kinesthetic/internal).

Each time a student recalls each of the above, he squeezes or presses his finger or wrist. Now, anytime the student wants to recall the positive state, he just squeezes or presses his finger or wrist and the good feelings return instantly.

THE STATE OF EXCELLENCE INTERVENTION

Ask the students if they remember a time when they were in a state of excellence. That is, a time when they really felt confident, calm, happy, strong, and so on. Draw an imaginary circle on the floor. Next, tell them to step into the circle and physically model what they look like in that state of excellence. As they physically demonstrate, tell them at the same time to think about that mental state of excellence.

Next, tell them to step outside of the circle and think of a time they felt "stuck" (tired, confused, unhappy, angry, etc.). As they begin to think of the stuck state, tell them to increase the negative feelings associated with the stuck state and to give you a signal (head nod) when they have almost peaked at the stuck state, just before the climax or peak, *not when they are into their feelings completely*.

When you see the signal, gently pull them into the circle of excellence and tell them to take on the posture of excellence. This intervention will reduce the negative feelings because it shows the relationship between physiology and emotions and demonstrates how altering physiology can control emotions.

We invite you to reflect:

Currently, how are you fostering resiliency in your children?
What would be different in your school if everyone believed that emotions influence understanding?
How do you begin the change?

Chapter Ten

Special Interventions to Shape Desirable Behavior

"Change has a considerable psychological impact on the human mind. To the fearful it is threatening because it means that things may get worse. To the hopeful it is encouraging because things may get better. To the confident it is inspiring because the challenge exists to make things better."

—King Whitney, Jr.

Key Points:

- Go for simple changes at first.
- "Use your brain for a change" (Richard Bandler).
- Set up the conditions for students to succeed.

This chapter focuses on additional interventions that work in concert with the students' brains to elicit behavioral change. Again, work with the mind in mind.

Teachers and administrators are always looking for practical solutions to the day-to-day challenges students present behaviorally. Unfortunately, many popular solutions are remedial, and tend to be ineffective with today's student. Ideally, a constructive and effective intervention or solution puts the child in control of his or her own behavior and raises his or her level of responsibility. Working from that point, sustainable behavioral change occurs.

The strategies that follow in this chapter are generative rather than remedial. They were developed, used, and refined over a period of ten years. We think most are helpful. In any event, our overriding philosophy is to try a strategy once or twice; if, in fact, it doesn't work, we try something else. (Please don't try the same interventions repeatedly if they fail to work.) The interventions take a little time to implement, but the time is worth it! Teachers can also defer to social workers or counselors if they feel they do not have sufficient time to devote to a specific intervention.

ANCHORING

Anchoring helps students redefine negative feelings into neutral ones. It is a technique from neurolinguistic programming, a unique communication model, which borrowed the concept from the stimulus and response psychology model.

Anchoring involves feelings and can be accomplished visually, auditorily, and/or kinesthetically. Negative feelings, as well as positive feelings, usually have the following path: They start from a neutral base, and, when one begins to think of the negative or positive situation, person, or thing, the feeling gradually (sometimes quickly) builds to a climax as illustrated by the drawing below.

Eventually, when one begins to stop thinking of the feeling, it gradually subsides into a neutral state. Anchoring helps students who continually find themselves in a negative frame of mind. Anchors are also helpful when a person constantly relives any troublesome situation. The goal is to offset the negative feelings by introducing positive feelings. These positive feelings are elicited from within the individual by the anchoring procedure.

Collapsing Anchors (Negative/Positive = Neutral)

1. Have student hold out his hand, resting it on his knees or a table. Have him choose one of the fingernails or knuckles on that hand that you can gently press. Have him think of the negative feeling, and when he senses the feeling is at its peak, tell him to nod his head. At the same time, press his fingernail or knuckle and hold it for about three seconds (anchoring the feeling to the finger).

2. Next, tell him to look to the left or right and then return to facing you. This is called a breaker state.
3. Using the fingernail or knuckle on the opposite hand, follow the same procedure as above, anchoring a positive or humorous feeling.
4. Next, have him break the state by turning to the left or right.
5. Now ask him to hold out both hands, allowing them to rest on the table or his knees.
6. Tell him to think of the negative feeling again and to nod his head when it reaches a climax. At the time the student reaches the negative climax and nods his head, press both the negative and positive anchors—only this time hold the negative for two seconds and let go. Continue to hold the positive anchor for four to five seconds.
7. To check whether the anchoring system worked, have him think of the negative feeling again or ask him to think into the future when he might encounter the negative feeling again. If the student says it's different now or it's neutralized, the anchor worked. If not, do the entire process over again until the negative feeling is neutralized.

As an additional note, it is sometimes recommended to anchor two separate positive anchors, if the negative anchor is strong.

Other Ways to Use Anchors in the Classroom

- Establish one place from which to give directions. This place is where important information is imparted.
- Establish one place where you give reprimands or admonish students. Don't contaminate the room by yelling in different places in the room. There can be a spot painted on the floor, for example. Tell the students that when you stand in this spot, someone is off task. Look directly at that student when on the spot.
- Establish an anchor to relieve anxiety before a test (i.e., point to a relaxing scene depicted in a wall poster, put on soothing music before a test is given, or create a group saying that puts students in a positive mood).
- Create a problem-solving space in the room. Send students there to solve problems or brainstorm possibilities. This is a possibility anchor.
- Use one kind of gesture or posture to bring students back to attention. (Remember when your teacher flicked the lights on and off?)

- Time-out locations can be created but should serve two purposes: one, to have students relax; and two, to have them *think about what to do differently*. Please don't ask students to sit there and think about what they did. That is not constructive.
- Establish a creative thinking spot where students can go to "create" new ideas or invent.
- Experiment with different volume levels and tones of voice. Try whispers or different rates of speech to elicit different reactions in students.

SWISHFUL THINKING

Many times students exhibit self-defeating behaviors. A positive self-concept is the result of empowering feelings and accepting yourself as you are. It's seeing the big picture and seeing you as you, not something you should be or that someone else wants you to be.

The Swishful Thinking exercise helps students handle blocks to a negative self-concept or self-defeating behaviors and enables students to see the positive aspects of themselves and life in general.

1. Have the student think of a time when he was down on himself. The student may also anticipate an event in the future about which he has negative feelings or fears of failure.
2. Have the student make an image of this unpleasantness and actually associate (see, hear, and feel) into the image, even if the feelings intensify. Have the student notice everything about the image.
3. Next, have the student look away to the right, then the left, one or two times or count from ten to one. This serves as a breaker state; in other words, it places a clear boundary between the two states.
4. Now, tell the student to create a resourceful self-image of himself the way he wants to be, as if:
   a. the negative situation has been resolved and he actually feels good about himself;
   b. the issue has been solved, and he has accomplished whatever it was that needed to be accomplished;
   c. he feels successful.
5. The student should create/project this "person," the successful person, in front of himself—a big, bright, and colorful image of him-

self. Then tell the student that this is the "new you" and that the new you feels good, feels light and wonderful. This new you, the wonderful image of you, is actually compelling you to want to be this person, and you hear positive comments coming from this new you. Tell the student to say, "I feel good; I am a good and resourceful person."

6. Next, have the student take the image and reduce it down to a small and brightly colored ball, one that can be moved around and made larger and larger.

7. The student is to take the small ball and place it in the center of the image, the negative image developed in step one.

8. Now the student takes the step one image and makes it slowly fade away as the small brightly colored ball gets bigger and brighter until the new wonderful and powerful you completely fills his mind's eye, and completely covers the negative step one image. Have the student hear himself say the positive comments as the positive image gets bigger and brighter.

9. Next, have the student clear his mind of what he just accessed by visualizing a blank screen in front of himself.

10. Now have the student repeat steps four through seven four more times, doing each repetition faster and faster.

11. Finally, tell him to try to get the original, unpleasant thought or image in his mind. If the experience of the step one image has changed or disappeared, he has been successful. If any unpleasant feelings or thoughts come back, repeat the process (steps four through seven) a few more times.

This exercise is a fascinating way to get students to create a more favorable and positive image of themselves and serves them well when they have to handle troublesome situations. The exercise forces them to think of who they really want to be or of how positively they want to appear, act, and feel in problem situations.

ELIMINATING FEARS/UNPLEASANT FEELINGS

A useful way to process unpleasant thoughts, feelings, and fears is to run them backward in one's mind. For most people, the following process, at a minimum, neutralizes these negative thoughts and feelings.

Unpleasant Memory

Have the student think of a fairly unpleasant memory and run a movie of it in her mind. As the student recalls the movie, tell her to listen to it as well and notice whatever unpleasant feelings come up. Run the movie from beginning to end.

Now have the student picture herself in the movie at the end and run the entire movie backward, in color and at high speed, taking only about three to five seconds. Be sure the student pretends she is inside the movie (associated) when it goes backward. Have the student do this at least three times. Then have the student run the movie that she first ran and tell the student to notice the feelings now.

Again, for most people the feelings should be neutralized at this point. Reliving the experience backward changes the order of the experience in one's mind; thus, the negative experience is altered. Be sure to tell the student that when the movie runs backward, it means everything is seen backward. All movements, talk, gestures, and scenes would appear just as videotape does when it runs in reverse.

WRITE, READ, AND RIP TECHNIQUE

This intervention allows students to objectify their problems, obsessions, and concerns. It can also decrease and eliminate troublesome thoughts, thus helping them to realize there are better things to do.

The process:

1. On Monday, Wednesday, and Friday, the student sits for one-half hour writing down all the good and bad memories about people or incidents that are upsetting to him or her.
2. On Tuesday, Thursday, and Sunday, the student reads what he or she wrote and rips up the notes and throws them away.
3. If unwanted thoughts occur, the student is to say, "I have better things to do now and I'll wait until my regular time comes to think about my problems/concerns/obsessions."

This strategy gets students to consciously "throw away" their problems or things that bother them.

STRUCTURED FIGHTS

(Structured Fights are for two individuals who constantly argue.)

1. Toss a coin to decide who will argue first.
2. The winner (A) gets to argue for five minutes, while the second student (B) listens without interrupting.
3. Then student B argues for five minutes, while student A listens.
4. Next, both students remain silent for five minutes of silence before another round starts with a coin toss.

Note: Sometimes it is best to have the students seated back-to-back while they argue.

NEW BEHAVIOR GENERATOR

The New Behavior Generator is a great intervention for those students who typically enjoy having power. As mentioned in chapter 4, this intervention meets "director" students in their model of the world. That said, we have found that this intervention works extraordinarily well with most children.

This is designed for students who repeatedly misbehave and haven't responded to typical interventions. Use the New Behavior Generator to go for small changes at first. Have the student practice the new behavior visually, auditorily, and kinesthetically once or twice, and then ask if this new behavior feels okay. This sensory-based process imprints the behavior in the student's mind.

Finally, if this doesn't work for the student, revise the plan and have the student repeat the process.

New Behavior Generator Process

1. Establish rapport.
2. Ask, "What did you do specifically?" (Get detailed information.)
3. Ask, "What rule did you violate?" (Fosters cause-and-effect thinking.)
4. Ask, "What can you do differently next time?" (Student brainstorms three ideas.)

  a.
  b.
  c.
5. Student picks one of the choices.
6. Student practices the new behavior, in his or her mind, visually, auditorily, and kinesthetically. Practice, practice, practice. Go for small changes at first. For example, if a student constantly talks, that student should attempt to sit quietly for ten minutes or so. Then, if successful, increase the amount of time to fifteen minutes the next time around. Always reward (verbally) positive changes.
7. Ask the student, "Are you going to do this?" (Get a commitment.)
8. Now, ask the student to imagine the next time he or she will be in the situation where he or she typically misbehaves. Tell them to see, here, and feel themselves performing the new behavior within that situation. Check for congruency (we refer to this as future-pacing.)
9. Revise the plan, if necessary.

And, lastly, with minor alterations, the New Behavior Generator can be used as a written contract.

Conclusion

After many years of working with troubled students, we have decided it is not necessary for teachers to know great details of a person's problem. All that is necessary is that the student in a problem situation *does* something different, even if the behavior is sometimes strange, irrational, or humorous.

The goal is not to dominate symptoms, but to help students set up conditions that will allow them to achieve their goals. Because someone's behavior is labeled as incorrect or inappropriate doesn't make it so. The same behavior in another context may be perfectly normal and acceptable. For example, a student may scream and yell in a classroom and that may not be acceptable in a normal context. However, when a student screams and yells in times of danger, his actions are not only acceptable, but also advisable.

In addition, we believe students really want to change their behavior; it is just that whatever they have tried hasn't worked. It is not that they are resistant as much as they get in their own way in most cases.

Finally, go for small changes at first. Small changes can sometimes make profound and extensive differences in the behaviors of people. As a last comment, these interventions presuppose a particular level of understanding of language. As we have stated often, you must meet people in their model of the world. So please adjust your language accordingly.

In remaining true to our belief in the power of stories, we choose to leave you with one. Just as the boy banging on his drum stopped when a master communicator asked him the right question, *"What's inside the drum?*," this story gives a nod to the idea of consultants of behavioral change remaining flexible and open, as well as maintaining a sense of humor.

Once upon a time, there was an elderly man who lived in a house on a corner. His corner lot had a fence around it. The house was on the way to an elementary school. It seemed like every day kids would come by and throw paper wrappers, soda cans, or schoolwork in his yard.

The man thought about confronting the young lads but didn't want to yell at them, as he didn't want them to be even more inconsiderate. One day he caught the boys going by his house. He said, "I know you are throwing stuff over the fence into my yard." The boys immediately denied they had ever done that.

The man continued, "I have seen you do it." The boys were about to run when the man said, "Wait a minute, I want you to throw stuff on my lawn." The young boys were puzzled. They thought he was crazy. The man said, "To show you I'm serious, I will give you one dollar for every day you throw your garbage into my yard." Now the boys knew the old man was crazy, but they said they would do it.

The next day, the boys tested the man. They threw papers over the fence. The man waited by the side of the house, came out, and gave them a dollar. He told them they did a good job and to keep doing it. This went on for two weeks.

After two weeks, the man met the young boys and said, "This is getting expensive, and I can't afford to pay you a dollar a day. I'll give you a quarter a day if you keep throwing your papers over the fence."

The boys responded, "Who do you think we are? We aren't going to do this for a quarter!" The man never had to clean up his yard again.

"And how are the children?" "The children are well; yes, all the children are well."

Reflection questions:

What had real meaning for you from what you've read?
What surprised you?
What challenged you?
What resonated with that which is boundless in you?

Bibliography and References

Bandler, R. *Using Your Brain—For a Change*. Moab, UT: Real People Press, 1985.

Bandler, R., & Grinder, J. *Reframing*. Moab, UT: Real People Press, 1982.

Bandler, R., & Grinder, J. *The Structure of Magic*. Palo Alto, CA: Science and Behavior Books, 1975.

Baumeister, R. F. et al. (1996). The Dark Side of Self Esteem. *Psychological Review*, 70–71

Blackerby, D. A. *Rediscover the Joy of Learning*. Oklahoma City, OK: Success Skills, 1996.

Costa, A., & Kallick, B. *Habits of Mind: A Developmental Series; Vol. 1. Discovering and Exploring Habits of Mind*. Alexandria, VA: Association for Supervision and Curriculum Development (ASCD), 2000.

Covey, Stephen. *The 7 Habits of Highly Effective People*. NY: Fireside, 1989.

Dennison, P. E., & Dennison, G. E. *Brain Gym*. Ventura, CA: Edu-Kinesthetics, 1989.

DePorter, B., & Hernacki, M. *Quantum Learning*. New York: Dell Publishing, 1992.

Dilts, R. B. *Applications of Neuro-Linguistic Programming*. Cupertino, CA: Meta Publications, 1983.

Dilts, R. B., & Epstein, T. L. *Dynamic Learning*. Capitola, CA: Meta Publications, 1995.

Dweck, C. *Mindset*. New York: Random House, 2006.

Erickson, M. *Life Reframing and Hypnosis*. New York: Irvington Publishers, 1985.

Feurstein, R. *Instrumental Enrichment: An Intervention Program for Cognitive Modifiability*. Glenview, IL: Scott, Foresman, 1980.

Hamer, D., & Copeland, P. *Living With Our Genes*. New York: Anchor Books, 1998.

Hannaford, C. *Smart Moves—Why Learning is not All in Your Head*. Arlington, VA: Great Ocean Publishers, 1995.

Heatherton, T. F., & Vohs, K. D. (2000). Personality Processes and Individual Differences—Interpersonal Evaluations Following Threats to Self: Role of Self Esteem. *Journal of Personality and Social Psychology*, 78, 725–36.

Hecht, D. *The Quick CLICK Survey*. Monroe Township, NJ: New Jersey Principals and Supervisors Association, 1996. http://www.search-institute.org/research/.

Kapp, S. *Guru: Metaphors from a Psychotherapist*. Palo Alto, CA: Science and Behavior Books, 1971.

Kohn, A. *Beyond Discipline: From Compliance to Community*. Alexandria, VA: ASCD, 1996.

Marx, G. *Ten Trends: Educating Children for a Profoundly Different Future*. Arlington, VA: Educational Research Service, 2000.

Myers, D. *Social Psychology* (7th ed.). New York: McGraw-Hill Higher Education, 2002.

Olsen, W., & Sommers, W. *A Trainer's Companion: Stories to Stimulate*. Highlands, TX: aha!Process, 2004.

Payne, R. *A Framework for Understanding Poverty*. Highlands, TX: aha!Process, 2003.

Pinker, S. *The Stuff of Thought*. New York: Viking, 2007.

Ready, R., & Burton, K. *Neuro-Linguistic Programming for Dummies*. Hoboken, NJ: John Wiley, 2004.

Robbins, A. *Awaken the Giant Within*. New York: Summit Books, 1991.

Rossi, E. L. *The 20 Minute Break; Using the New Science of ULTRADIAN RHYTHMS*. New York: St. Martin's Press, 1991.

Scannella, A. *Changing Student Behavior: Comprehensive Learning for Correcting Kids*. Lanham, MD: Rowman & Littlefield Education, 2007.

Scannella, A., and Webster-O'Dell, W. (Eds.). *The Children We Share*. Monroe Township, NJ: The Foundation for Educational Administration and the New Jersey Principals and Supervisors Association, 2003.

Siler, T. *Think Like a Genius*. New York: Bantam Books, 1999.

Simon, R. (Ed.). (2007, March/April). The Top Ten. *Psychotherapy Networker,* *31*, 24–37, 68.

Sousa, D. A. *How the Brain Learns*. Reston, VA: National Association of Secondary School Principals, 1995.

Sylwester, R. *Biological Brain in a Cultural Classroom: Applying Biological Research to Classroom Management*. Thousand Oaks, CA: Corwin Press, 2000.

Van Nagel, C. et al. *Megateaching and Learning*. Indian Rock Beach, FL: Southern Institute Press, 1985.

Wolfe, P. *Brain Matters—Translating Research into Classroom Practice.* Alexandria, VA: ASCD, 2001.

Yeager, J. *Thinking About Thinking with NLP.* Capitola, CA: Meta Publications, 1985.

Zander, B., & Zander, R. *The Art of Possibility.* Boston: Harvard Business School Press, 2000.

About the Authors

Dr. Anthony Scannella is chief executive officer of the Foundation for Educational Administration, Inc. (FEA). Prior to this, Dr. Scannella served as the director of professional development for the New Jersey Principals and Supervisors Association. Dr. Scannella, a former principal, assistant principal, director of curriculum, and psychotherapist, is the author of a number of notable education projects and texts including *Sending the Right Signals*, a program to eliminate sexual harassment; coauthor of *The Children We Share*, a program for parents and principals; and the author of *Changing Student Behavior: Comprehensive Learning and Interventions for Correcting Kids*. Dr. Scannella has trained at the state, national, and international levels and currently conducts a yearly leadership conference held on the campus of Princeton, which attracts school leaders from throughout the United States and abroad. He received his doctorate from Rutgers University in 1982 and in 1998 received the Distinguished Educator Award from the Rutgers Graduate School of Education for outstanding and exemplary service in his field.

Sharon McCarthy established ENVISION: Breakthroughs in Learning, a training and consulting firm in New Jersey, in 2000. Through ENVISION, she consults and conducts seminars and workshops with schools, businesses, and agencies on topics such as mediating cognitive structures for improved learning and behavior; acquisition of skills for formal, informal, and youth leadership; using the brain to increase memory; positive human relations through master communication; and care of the self. Her workshops always receive positive feedback. A popular workshop is her Parent University, a multiday training that teaches parents how to assist their children, both behaviorally and academically.

One of Sharon's specialties is working with teachers, parents, and administrators to assist underachieving students of all levels and ages. She works with them in two primary areas: teaching them how to learn and positively affecting their attitudes about school and learning. She also works with students with learning disabilities, including attention deficit disorder (ADD).

Sharon draws upon her background as a parent, coach, educator, and neurolinguistic programming (NLP) master practitioner to create powerful interventions that address specific school and student issues.

For information on trainings and seminars, please contact ENVISION at ienvision@mac.com or 732.714.7688.